DON'T WORRY, YOU'RE NORMAL

DON'T WORRY,
You're Normal
A TEENAGER'S GUIDE TO SELF-HEALTH
NISSA SIMON

Thomas Y. Crowell
New York

For
Rob, Jonea, and Andrea
    ... with love

Library of Congress Cataloging in Publication Data

Simon, Nissa.
    Don't worry, you're normal.
    Summary: A health guide discussing such topics as
growth of the body, nutrition, skin care, drug use, and
sex.
    1. Health—Juvenile literature. 2. Youth—Health
and hygiene—Juvenile literature. [1. Health.
2. Grooming] I. Title.
RA777.S52 1982   613'.0433   81-43324
ISBN 0-690-04138-1   AACR2
ISBN 0-690-04139-X (lib. bdg.)
        4 5 6 7 8 9 10

CONTENTS

ACKNOWLEDGMENTS

I would like to thank the following people, all of whom took time from already busy schedules to read drafts of the manuscript and offer valuable comments:

George Christakis, M.D., M.P.H., chief, Nutrition Division, Department of Epidemiology and Public Health, University of Miami School of Medicine;

Edmund Crelin, Ph.D., D.Sc., professor of anatomy, Yale University School of Medicine;

Alan Goodman, M.D., associate clinical professor of orthopedic surgery, Yale University School of Medicine;

Ernest Hartmann, M.D., professor of psychiatry, Tufts University School of Medicine and director, Sleep Research Laboratory, West Ros-Park Mental Health Center, Boston;

Sidney Hurwitz, M.D., associate clinical professor of pediatrics and dermatology, Yale University School of Medicine;

Herbert Kleber, M.D., professor of psychiatry, Yale University School of Medicine and director, Substance Abuse Treatment Unit, Connecticut Mental Health Center;
Remy Lazarowicz, assistant director, VD National Hotline;
Saul Milles, M.D., associate clinical professor of medicine, Yale University School of Medicine;
Mary Jane Minkin, M.D.;
Jerome Serling, D.D.S., director, Family Dentistry Residency Program, University of Connecticut School of Dental Medicine;
Sidney Spiesel, M.D., assistant professor of pediatrics, Yale University School of Medicine,
and especially to my children, and to their friends, for their valuable editorial services.

INTRODUCTION

Your teen years are a time of transition between childhood
and adulthood. Because they are years of rapid physical and
psychological change, they have unique characteristics. Perhaps at no other time of your life will you have more questions about your body than during this period. Yet these are
the years when you sometimes hesitate to state your concerns
because you don't want to admit that you don't know. Or
you find it difficult to discuss specific subjects because you
think you may shock the person you're talking to. You sometimes believe that you're the only one who's ever felt the way
you do. And, if you do talk about a problem, you're often
told that you're "going through a stage."

Until recently, doctors treated teenagers as if they were

nothing more than large children when it came to medical care. Most doctors now recognize that teenagers are a distinct group with special needs—and medical treatment and research take this into consideration. As a teenager, however, you often don't have access to the newest information concerning your health, because finding the facts is difficult. It takes a long time for new developments to make their way into textbooks, so what you read in school may be dated and perhaps inaccurate. Magazine articles do present current material, but not always on the specific subjects you want to read about.

The purpose of this book is to give you correct information, based on the most recent medical research, about the physical and psychological changes teenagers experience. There are chapters on such things as nutrition, skin, hair, sleep, and posture. This book also covers growth, infectious diseases, drug use, sexual questions, emotional concerns, and what to expect from a doctor/patient relationship. These particular topics were chosen because they were considered important by a large group of teenagers, most of whom believed that there wasn't enough information available to them about these subjects. As a writer who specializes in medical subjects, I felt that this material could be presented in a way all teenagers could understand.

Medical researchers discover new facts almost daily. Each chapter in this book is based on the newest information available, and was checked for accuracy by doctors and researchers working in the specific area. There are many books for teenagers on individual subjects concerning their health. As far as I know, this is the only book to cover all these topics from a medical point of view in a single volume.

The teen years are the years when you start to take more responsibility for your own well-being, health, and appearance. This book is meant to help you do that.

GROWTH AND
SEXUAL DEVELOPMENT

Adolescence starts with the period of growth called puberty. Puberty is the time when you mature physically and usually starts when girls are about ten years old and boys are about twelve. But these are *average* ages, and individuals vary greatly. You can start puberty much earlier or much later and still be normal.

As you go through puberty, your childhood patterns of height and weight gain change markedly. Typically, you grow slowly and evenly until the rapid changes known as "the adolescent growth spurt." Suddenly, you start growing taller and gaining weight quickly. This is the time when teenagers may become clumsy, knocking over tables and tripping over chairs, and often seem to be all hands and feet.

I

Clumsiness is a result of rapid growth—you haven't yet adjusted to dealing with your longer arms and legs. This is also the time when you grow out of the shoes . . . the shirt . . . the jeans . . . the coat . . . that you bought just three months ago . . . two months ago . . . last month.

The adolescent growth spurt lasts for about two years. Both boys and girls often grow eight inches during this time. So it's not surprising that you grow into and out of your clothes so quickly. After this period of rapid, extensive change, your body slows down again; height and weight continue to increase at a slower rate until you're about eighteen years old. At that time, most of your growth is complete —you'll have only about an inch more of height left to grow.

The age at which adolescent growth starts will differ from person to person, but there is an order in which changes occur that's usually the same for everyone. During this period, almost every part of the body, internal as well as external, changes. The heart increases in size and the digestive tract enlarges, as do the liver, kidneys, and spleen.

Some of the most obvious changes are changes in your bones. The bones in the arms and legs usually grow longer first, and then the shoulders and hips become broader. (In boys, shoulders become broader than hips, while in girls, shoulders and hips become about equal in width.) Finally, the bones of the spine, which control the length of the trunk, grow longer. Your increase in height is the result of the lengthening of both your trunk and your legs. During this time, your facial bones also grow and change, so your looks may change more rapidly.

As the skeleton changes, muscles also change in size and strength. Before puberty, boys and girls are about equal in strength. Girls seem to stop increasing in strength at about the time they start menstruating, but muscle growth in boys continues until about two years after the rapid gain in height. Individual muscle cells increase in size in both boys and girls, but in boys the number of muscle cells also increases. By the time growth ends, boys have about 10 percent more muscle in relation to body weight than girls.

Before the growth spurt begins, boys and girls also have the same amount of body fat. Body fat accumulates slowly during childhood until it reaches about 15 percent of total weight. At puberty, the amount of body fat that boys have remains the same. But the proportion of body fat decreases as they increase in height and muscle mass. The amount of body fat girls have increases at puberty. At the end of adolescent growth, about 10 percent of a boy's weight is made up of fat tissue, while about 20 percent of a girl's weight is made up of fat tissue.

At the same time that body height and weight are changing, the reproductive organs are developing rapidly. This sexual maturation is under the direction of the pituitary gland, which releases hormones called gonadotropins.

Hormones are chemical signals that circulate throughout the body and regulate many bodily functions, including how and when to grow (and when to stop), and how to retain its own chemical balance. There are at least fifty different hormones that we know about at present that are produced by the endocrine system (a complex network of glands that release hormones directly into the bloodstream).

At puberty, the pituitary gland sends out two different hormone signals among others. FSH, follicle-stimulating hormone, stimulates the ovaries in girls to produce eggs, and the testes in boys to produce sperm. LH, luteinizing hormone, stimulates the ovaries to produce estrogen and progesterone, female hormones, and the testes to produce testosterone, a male hormone. As the body steps up its production of testosterone or progesterone and estrogen, the reproductive organs and other sex characteristics change and develop.

Probably the first sign of the start of puberty in boys is that the testes enlarge, though the penis and the rest of the body look the same. Usually boys have two testes; they are the glands that hang under the penis, encased in a skin sac called the scrotum. It's normal for one testis to hang somewhat lower than the other. Usually both testes descend from the body after birth. Sometimes, either one or both testes don't descend into the scrotum, and sometimes boys are born with only one testis. Neither condition usually interferes with the ability to father children or with the ability to enjoy sex.

As the testes enlarge, so does the scrotum. As the scrotum grows, the skin changes from smooth to wrinkled. At the same time, pubic hair starts to grow. Pubic hair, hair around the sex organs, is the first hair associated with sexual development. The first pubic hairs are likely to be fine and straight, but pubic hair will become coarse and curly as development continues. At about this time, hair also begins to appear under the arms and above the upper lip. Eventually boys grow hair on the chin and along the jawline, and finally on the neck. At the same time, the voice starts to deepen as the larynx becomes larger and the vocal cords grow longer and thicker. These changes are influenced by an increase in the level of testosterone.

The penis, which is made up of spongy tissue and blood vessels, starts to grow longer and broader some time after the testes have enlarged. When blood rushes into the penis faster than it leaves it, the spongy tissue expands because it is under pressure from the extra blood. The penis becomes hard and stands away from the body, erect. This is called an erection or "hard-on." As blood flow to the penis is reduced, the erection subsides.

Boys usually compare penis size and wonder about someone else who has either a larger penis or a smaller one. In a mature male, average penis size, without an erection, is three to four inches long and about an inch and a quarter in diameter. But there are variations, and the size of your penis when it's flaccid (non-erect) has little to do with how large it will be when it's erect. With an erection, a smaller penis often "grows" quite a bit in size, while a large penis may not get much larger.

When erect, the average penis is just over six inches long. The size of your penis has nothing to do with how often you'll have an erection, or how many ejaculations you'll be able to have in a given length of time. Neither does it have anything to do with how much you'll enjoy sex, because sensation during sexual intercourse is the same regardless of penis size.

Teenage boys commonly get spontaneous erections—that is, erections that happen suddenly, without any warning, and usually when you least expect them. Erections usually occur when you're sexually aroused, but many boys and men find that a full bladder stimulates an erection, and tight clothing or underpants that rub may also cause them. Spontaneous erections are more frequent in adolescence than in adulthood; you'll have fewer as you get older. There's no way to keep spontaneous erections from happening, and they'll subside on their own. You'll probably be more comfortable if you wear close-fitting jockey shorts during your teenage years. And remember, these erections feel more obvious to you than they look to others.

Sometimes your testes hang loose in the scrotum, and sometimes muscle tissue in the skin of the scrotum contracts, causing the scrotum to tighten up and hold the testes up against your body. This happens because the job of the scrotum is to keep the testes at the right temperature to produce sperm. Sperm are generally produced at a temperature a few degrees lower than body temperature, so, usually, your testes are kept away from the body, where they can remain cooler. In cold weather, however, the scrotum tightens up so that the testes can get more warmth.

Immature sperm cells are present in your testes from birth, and start to mature at puberty. After puberty, more sperm are constantly being produced, so you won't run out of them. The sperm travel through a series of ducts. The first duct, called the epididymis, lies tightly coiled over the testis. The sperm then go to the vas deferens, a continuation of the epididymis, where they're stored until ejaculation.

The seminal vesicles and the prostate gland, which lies below the bladder, make a milky white fluid called semen. During an orgasm, sperm mixed with semen is ejaculated from the body. Your body starts to produce semen (or "come") about a year after your testes and penis start to grow. When the muscles in your penis contract during an ejaculation, the semen is pushed out in spurts. (Incidentally, you can't urinate at the same time that you are ejaculating, because nerves controlling urination inhibit the release of urine.)

The ability to ejaculate semen means that you've matured sexually. Sometimes a boy realizes this has happened only when he wakes in the morning and finds his pajama bottoms sticky and wet. He has ejaculated during the night. This is called having a "wet dream," technically known as a nocturnal emission.

Nocturnal emissions, the release of semen during sleep, are

perfectly normal. Most boys have them; they're usually associated with dreams that have a sexual content, but not always. Boys who masturbate have fewer wet dreams than boys who don't, because wet dreams are the body's way of relieving a buildup of sperm in the testes. There's a wide variation in the frequency of wet dreams, and many boys worry that they'll run out of sperm if they have them often. This won't happen, because the body constantly produces more sperm.

Adolescent boys sometimes notice that their breasts are enlarging. This is a common condition called gynecomastia, and it affects about three-quarters of all boys at some time during puberty. The enlargement usually doesn't become as noticeable as the enlargement of a girl's breasts, and is generally confined to the area under the areola (the darker, central nipple area). Gynecomastia is probably due to a passing imbalance of hormones during early puberty. Although it's frightening for a boy to see his breasts start to enlarge, it doesn't mean that he's less masculine or that he'll have noticeable breasts all his life. Gynecomastia is a normal phenomenon; in most cases, the condition subsides within a year without any treatment. If you're concerned about it, have your doctor check it. Recently, some cases of gynecomastia have been linked to heavy marijuana usage, probably because of the effect of marijuana on hormone levels. If the breasts don't return to normal size with time, the excess tissue can be removed surgically with excellent results.

In girls, the first sign that puberty has begun is development of the breasts. Visible breast development starts anywhere from one to two years before menstruation begins. Often, breast development will be uneven, with one breast developing more rapidly than the other. It's important to know that this is not abnormal or dangerous. No paired organs are ever absolutely identical, so one breast will never be exactly the same as the other, though they'll eventually look the same size. Everyone is asymmetrical, and one side of the body will always differ from the other a little bit.

At the same time that the breasts begin to grow, the areola (the darker portion around the nipple) enlarges, and the fat cells that form most of the breast tissue start to grow in size. Your body's own genetic code determines the eventual size of your breasts, and that's the only thing that does. Exercise will improve posture so that your bustline has a better contour, but there are no exercises, massages, moisturizing lotions, or massage creams that will help to enlarge small breasts. Don't waste your money on them, no matter how convincing the advertisements sound.

The size of your breasts doesn't have anything to do with whether you can breast-feed babies or not, as some girls think. Women with small breasts can nurse babies as well as women with large breasts, because the ability to produce milk has nothing to do with breast size.

Usually the breasts start enlarging before pubic hair begins to appear. As in boys, when pubic hair does appear, it's straight and fine at first. In girls, the first pubic hair appears on the labia majora, the outer lips of the genitals. As puberty progresses, pubic hair darkens and becomes more curly, and leg and underarm hair starts to appear.

Girls' genitals aren't as visible as boys', but you can see yours if you use a hand mirror. The entire area between a girl's legs is called the vulva, meaning "external genitals." The outer lips, the labia majora, protect the genital area and generally meet. If you spread them, you'll see the inner lips, the labia minora. Sometimes the inner lips extend below the outer ones. The labia minora can vary in color and can be wrinkled or smooth. All these variations are normal.

The labia minora come together at the front to surround the clitoris, the center of sexual sensation in girls and women and, in this way, the female equivalent of the penis. Below the clitoris is the urethra, the opening for urine. Below the urethra is the vaginal opening that leads to the vagina. Sometimes—but rarely—the vaginal opening is completely blocked by a hymeneal membrane that is present in all females during early development before birth. Normally, this membrane disappears before a girl is born, though a ring of tissue may persist. This ring of tissue is commonly, but erroneously, called the hymen. People used to think that if this tissue ring tore and bled during sexual intercourse, it was a definite sign that a girl was a virgin—and that if this did not happen, it meant a girl had had intercourse before. We now know that many girls are born with only a small amount of this tissue ring, so that it may not tear and bleed during first intercourse. Therefore, the absence of bleeding is no indication that a girl is not a virgin.

The vaginal opening connects your external genitals to your internal ones. Inside the opening is the vagina, the passage to the cervix, the lower part of the uterus. A small dimple in the center of the cervix is called the os; this is the opening through which menstrual flow passes. The os can open wide enough to allow a baby to pass through during childbirth. Unless you're about to deliver a baby, however, the os remains tiny, and the cervix closes off the upper end of the vagina. There's no way for anything, such as a tampon, to get lost inside of you.

The uterus, or womb, is a pear-shaped muscular organ where a fertilized egg can grow and develop into a fetus. There are two uterine tubes, one at each side of the uterus, that lead to the ovaries. (You may have heard these tubes referred to as Fallopian tubes, or oviducts, the old terms for them.)

Each month, the ovaries secrete an increasing amount of estrogen. This ultimately triggers the pituitary gland to send out FSH (follicle-stimulating hormone) into the bloodstream. The FSH in turn stimulates one egg cell to grow in one of the ovaries. The follicle cells surrounding the egg cell itself produce estrogen. While the egg cell is growing, the lining of the uterus, or endometrium, is stimulated by the estrogen to develop and thicken so that it can nourish a fertilized egg if one should eventually pass into the uterus.

About two weeks after this cycle (the menstrual cycle) starts, the amount of FSH in the bloodstream decreases and a large amount of LH (luteinizing hormone) is released by the pituitary gland. This causes the mature egg to be released from the follicle (egg capsule), and the egg starts traveling down the connecting uterine tube toward the uterus. The cells of the follicle itself now take on a different form and function. The follicle becomes the corpus luteum, or "yellow body," and its cells produce the hormone progesterone. This hormone stimulates the endometrium further, preparing it to nourish a fertilized egg.

If the egg isn't fertilized by sperm, the corpus luteum breaks down, and the levels of estrogen and progesterone in the blood decrease. This causes the endometrium to stop growing. Two or three days later, the unneeded endometrial tissue, along with the remains of the disintegrated egg cell, begin to pass out of the uterus and into the vagina. They are passed out of the body in the form of menstrual flow.

All girls and women menstruate after they reach puberty unless they are pregnant or there is some physical problem. The two terms generally used in referring to the process of menstruation are menstrual period and menstrual cycle. They are not the same thing. Your menstrual period is the time during which the unneeded endometrial lining is sloughed off, and it usually lasts from three to five days. Your menstrual cycle is the continuous process of releasing an egg that has matured (ovulation), building up a new lining in the uterus for the egg, and finally shedding the unneeded lining and the disintegrating egg. An average cycle is twenty-eight days—the time from the start of one menstrual period to the start of the next. But cycles vary from person to person, so your average cycle can be twenty-one days or thirty-five days or even forty-five days and still be normal. Illnesses and stress can influence the length of a cycle, and it's not at all unusual for cycles to be irregular for the first few years you menstruate.

Some girls find that they start having menstrual cramps (dysmenorrhea) after their cycles become regular. Contrary to what well-meaning but misinformed people may tell you, *cramps are not in your head.* They are not caused by poor posture, emotions, or lack of exercise. Nor do cramps mean that something's wrong physically. Scientists now believe that cramps are caused by an oversecretion of prostaglandins, chemicals produced in your body that resemble hormones. An oversecretion of prostaglandins causes the uterus to contract vigorously; this interferes with blood circulation and produces pain.

Aspirin is a weak prostaglandin inhibitor, and may help relieve cramps. If you're not allergic to aspirin and if it doesn't cause an upset stomach, try taking two aspirin tablets every three to four hours when you have cramps. If you can't take aspirin, a substitute such as Tylenol may help. Other over-the-counter pills for menstrual cramps, such as Midol, work well for some girls. And there are some old-fashioned remedies for menstrual cramps that may work for you. A heating pad or a hot bath and a hot drink have been used for generations to relieve cramps, and sometimes they may be all that's needed. (By the way, there's no reason to avoid tub baths during your period if you like them better than showers.) If none of these remedies help, your doctor may want to prescribe a stronger prostaglandin inhibitor to ease uterine contractions. Most doctors today try to avoid prescribing oral contraceptives to control menstrual cramps. Though the Pill nearly always works, it changes the hormone balance in the body—which may not be good for a teenage girl whose menstrual cycle isn't yet established.

When it comes to growth, "average" does *not* mean the same thing as "normal." Everyone grows at an individual rate, usually determined by genes inherited from parents. "Normal" development can be well ahead of or behind the "average." Most charts giving average ages of body change don't take into account individual differences, and they may cause a lot of undue worry. Your age in years is a poor standard when it comes to evaluating your physical development. For instance, the average age for a boy to start a spurt of growth in height is fourteen—but any time between age ten and a half and age sixteen is considered normal. The average age for a girl to start a spurt of growth in height is twelve, but girls can start growing any time between age nine and a half and age fourteen and a half and still be normal.

Because the rate of development varies, individual boys and girls of the same age show different degrees of physical maturity. Doctors therefore now use a standardized rating based on development, not age. These maturity ratings, when used together with measures such as bone development, can give your doctor information about how much more you're likely to grow in height and weight, and where you are in terms of sexual development. If you're at all concerned about physical differences between you and friends of yours, make an appointment to talk to your doctor about it.

Everyone who's ever been a teenager or is a teenager now —including your friends who seem so sure of themselves— has worried about some aspect of his or her physical development at some time or another during puberty. It's normal to worry—but it's rare for anything to be seriously wrong.

NUTRITION

During your teen years, your body is changing in more ways and more rapidly than at any other time of life except infancy. These changes come about so quickly that they can be alarming, though they're perfectly normal.

Not many teenagers are satisfied with their weight. Most think they're either too fat or too thin, or that the fat that's there is in all the wrong places. If you feel this way, you've probably tried dieting. Maybe you've tried a natural-food diet, a grapefruit diet, a no-carbohydrate diet—some diet that promises to get you down (or up) to what you'd like to weigh.

But what you'd *like* to weigh and what you *should* weigh aren't necessarily the same, and you can't tell if you're the right weight just by getting on a scale. The right weight for you depends on your height, your build, and your ratio of fat to lean body mass. (Lean body mass is everything except fat.)

Before adolescence, boys and girls have about the same ratio of fat to lean body mass. After puberty, boys undergo a rapid spurt in muscle growth and end up with about 10 percent total body fat. Girls, on the other hand, wind up with about 20 percent. Being overweight means having too much body fat in relation to lean body mass.

One precise way of measuring body fat is to be weighed under water in a specially designed tank. Because these tanks are scarce, a simpler way of figuring fat ratio has been devised. It uses "skin calipers" to measure skin-fold thickness. Many doctors and athletic coaches know how to take these measurements. A very rough measure you can try yourself is to stand straight and pinch the skin at your waistline between your thumb and index finger. If your fingers are spread more than an inch apart, you're probably carrying around too much fat.

Because charts that state average weight and height for your age are the least accurate measure of overweight and underweight, you should use them only as a rough guideline. The following chart shows the height and weight range for 90 percent of all boys and girls from ten to seventeen; 5 percent fall below the lower figure and 5 percent are above. For each age, half the boys or girls are below the mid-point figure and half are above.

All of this is likely to be confusing unless you understand just what extra fat is and why it gets added. If you have extra

GIRLS

Age	Height in Inches			Weight in Pounds		
	From	To	Mid-point	From	To	Mid-point
10	50.2	58.9	54.4	53.6	103.8	71.6
11	52.6	61.5	57.0	59.9	118.8	81.3
12	55.0	64.1	59.6	67.1	133.8	91.4
13	57.2	66.2	61.9	75.1	148.1	101.4
14	58.5	67.4	63.1	83.1	160.8	110.6
15	59.3	68.0	63.7	90.2	171.1	118.1
16	59.7	68.2	63.9	95.5	178.2	123.0
17	60.1	68.3	64.2	98.4	181.4	124.7

BOYS

Age	Height in Inches			Weight in Pounds		
	From	To	Mid-point	From	To	Mid-point
10	50.3	58.3	54.1	53.5	99.6	69.2
11	52.2	61.0	56.4	59.0	113.2	77.7
12	54.2	63.9	58.9	65.7	127.8	87.5
13	56.3	66.9	61.6	74.0	143.0	98.9
14	58.6	69.6	64.2	84.1	158.7	111.7
15	61.1	71.6	66.5	94.8	174.1	123.6
16	63.4	73.0	68.3	105.0	188.4	136.6
17	64.9	73.7	69.4	113.3	200.9	145.9

fat, it can be one of two kinds. Either you have a normal number of fat cells that have become overstuffed, or you have too many fat cells.

The type of fat cell you have and, therefore, the way you put on extra fat is determined by the genes you've inherited from your parents. This doesn't mean that you won't be able to lose weight if your parents are overweight, or that you'll stay overweight "because it runs in the family." It does mean that the way you lose weight depends on the type of fat cell you have. If you have a normal number of fat cells that have become overstuffed, they'll shrink to normal size when you lose weight. If you have too many fat cells, each cell will go to below-normal size when you lose weight.

The kind of excess fat that comes from having too many fat cells is a more serious problem, because once the fat cells are there, they will never disappear. You'll probably want to be careful about putting on weight during adolescence, because one theory has it that this is one of two times in your life when you can accumulate extra fat cells very easily. (The other time is during infancy.)

No matter which type of fat you have, if it's become a problem to you, it's because you've eaten more food than you have burned as energy. In other words, you've eaten more calories than you need.

Everyone knows that cake has more calories than celery. But just what is a calorie? People on diets tend to think of calories as a measure of potential fat, but they really are a measure of potential energy. A calorie is a way of measuring the amount of energy (in the form of heat) that the body can produce from a food substance.

When food is digested, it is used by the body as fuel to generate the energy the body runs on. (Just as an engine runs on gasoline, your body runs on food.) If you eat more food than you burn to provide energy, the extra potential energy is stored in the form of fat—ready to be used if needed.

All food contains calories, and some foods contain more than others. If you eat fewer calories than you burn as energy, you'll lose weight. Each pound of fat in your body contains about 3,500 calories. To gain a pound of weight, you must eat 3,500 more calories than you use for energy. To lose a pound of weight, you must, conversely, use up 3,500 calories more than you eat.

You need fifteen calories a day for each pound of weight just to maintain your weight as it is. The best way to lose weight is to eat enough of the nutrients you need to stay healthy, but to *cut down drastically* on the concentrated-calorie foods like fats, refined sugars, and refined carbohydrates. This is not to say you must eliminate these foods altogether. If you can cut down only 500 calories a day (for instance, one Big Mac, or two pieces of Kentucky-fried chicken, or one large soft-ice-cream cone), you'll lose a pound a week.

You have to be able to do more than count calories if you want to stay healthy and lose weight at the same time—you have to understand something about nutrition. With some knowledge of nutrition, you'll be able to sort out the foods you need from the ones you can safely do without.

Because your body is changing so rapidly during adolescence, you need more food than you did as a child. Though the exact requirements vary from person to person, there are basic substances in food called "nutrients" that every human body needs. Five of these nutrients are necessary to life: proteins, carbohydrates, fats, vitamins, and minerals. Most foods contain a mixture. Milk, for example, is rich in calcium (a mineral) but also contains vitamins A and D, carbohydrates, and fat. We can also measure potential energy in a glass of milk—that is, the number of calories it contains: 170 calories in a glass of whole milk, 85 calories in a glass of skim milk.

Without protein, you can't grow. It's as simple as that. Protein provides the building blocks for muscles, blood, skin, hair, bone—in fact, for every part of the body except fat. There are three sources of protein: animal, vegetable, and dairy. The protein in all of them can be broken down into substances called amino acids. There are twenty amino acids that we know about, and the body can manufacture most of the needed ones from the carbohydrates you eat. There are nine, however, called the "essential amino acids," that must be obtained directly from the food you eat, because the body cannot make them.

Sources of animal protein, as well as dairy products such

as milk and cheese, contain the essential amino acids, and so are considered "complete protein" foods. Some vegetables contain some of the essential amino acids and are "incomplete protein" foods. Eating the right combinations of vegetable proteins can supply all the essential amino acids.

The only way to insure that you're getting enough protein is to eat a variety of foods. The body doesn't store extra protein as such. It converts most of the excess to fat and stores it that way.

Carbohydrates are starches and sugars that are digested rapidly and converted to glucose (a kind of sugar). The body breaks down the glucose to yield energy and to enable the brain to function. Carbohydrates are present in grains and vegetables as starch, and in fruits as sugar.

If the body isn't getting enough carbohydrates from the diet to produce the glucose it needs, it will convert some protein and fat into glucose. That's why it's important to eat enough of the right kinds of carbohydrates—otherwise protein that should be used to build and repair muscle will be converted to glucose to keep the brain functioning.

Carbohydrates supply about three-quarters of the daily calories of people who live in cultures where rice is the major staple food. Most of these people are not overweight, because their carbohydrates come from natural, unrefined foods—they're eating a considerable amount of carbohydrate without taking in too many calories.

Refined carbohydrates are something else. Refining is a

mechanical process that changes the food from its original form, usually stripping bulk and nutrients and leaving a concentrated sugar or starch. Table sugar is the principal refined carbohydrate in American diets.

Everyone in this country eats too much refined sugar. We each consume about 120 pounds a year. To visualize how much that is, picture twenty-four five-pound bags of sugar sitting on a table. That's how much you eat each year if your diet is typical.

Things that have a lot of sugar in them, like cakes, candies, soft drinks, and pies, are said to contain "empty calories," because sugar doesn't supply any of the nutrients necessary to the body. And the calories in sugar add up quickly. One teaspoonful contains about fifteen calories. You'd have to hike a mile just to burn up the calories in four teaspoons of sugar!

It would be easy to get an entire day's worth of calories by eating four pieces of devil's food cake with frosting. But you'd get no protein and very few necessary vitamins and minerals in that cake. The calories would be in the form of refined carbohydrates and fat.

Some people think they can avoid the empty calories in sugar by using honey instead. They're wrong. Honey, brown sugar, maple sugar, corn syrup, and molasses are all sugars; all have about the same number of calories, and all are digested by the body in the same way. The difference in vitamin and mineral content among them is so small it hardly makes a difference. Molasses does contain some minerals, including iron and calcium, but these are available in other foods with many fewer calories.

Sugar is supposed to supply quick energy—or so the commercials say. Refined sugar probably has the opposite effect, however. The pancreas has to pour out insulin to cope with the large amount of sugar in a candy bar, for instance, so your body gets a jolt. But after the sugar is digested—which happens very quickly—you're usually left feeling more exhausted than before. If you eat a candy bar because you're feeling tired, you may find you've taken in a lot of calories and feel worse in the end.

The moderate amount of fat that you need in your diet provides energy and helps with the absorption of the fat-soluble vitamins: A, D, E, and K. When fat is digested, it carries these vitamins along into your bloodstream. After fat reaches the bloodstream, some is burned as energy; the rest is stored, to be used in the future.

Foods rich in fat have more calories than the same amount of almost any other food—usually more than twice as many calories, in fact. If you eat a lot of fat in your diet, no matter what kind, you're eating a lot of calories. Different kinds of fats—vegetable oil, margarine, butter, lard, animal fat—all have approximately the same number of calories per tablespoon.

Vitamins help to convert food to living tissue, and help us to utilize the energy in food. Vitamins are organic substances not manufactured by the body. Minerals are inorganic compounds that contribute to energy production and body maintenance. Why vitamins and minerals work is still a mystery, even to scientists. But every vitamin that's been discovered so far plays a specific role in keeping you healthy, as does every mineral that's been identified as necessary to humans. (See the chart at the end of this chapter to learn about specific vitamins and minerals and how the body uses them.)

What about taking vitamin pills?

Vitamin and mineral supplements contain varying amounts of the substances known to be necessary for good health. Still, we don't know why some of the minerals are necessary, or whether all the vitamins that are present in our food have been discovered yet. Much of the research now being done stresses the interactions among vitamins and minerals—that is, how each influences the others. Because the body is so finely tuned, it may be easy to upset the balance between vitamins and minerals by taking a large amount of any single one. Taking a balanced supplement won't do any harm, and it may do some good—but it won't make up for a poor diet.

How can you make sure you're eating the things you need for healthy skin and hair, for growth and for energy, and still control your weight? By eating a balanced diet. You've probably heard much more than you ever wanted to about a balanced diet. But here it is again, because it's essential for your continued health.

Food can be classified into these basic groups:

1.   PROTEIN FOODS: meat and poultry of all kinds, fish, eggs, peanut butter, dried beans and peas, and cheese. The ideal diet contains two servings a day from this group.

2.   CARBOHYDRATE FOODS: bread, beans, rice, potatoes, and cereal. The ideal diet contains four servings a day from this group.

3.   FRUITS AND VEGETABLES: all of them. The ideal diet contains four servings a day from this group.

4.   MILK AND DAIRY PRODUCTS: cheese (again), yogurt, cottage cheese, ice cream, and, of course, milk. The ideal diet contains three to four servings a day from this group (but the servings should not all be ice cream, because it's got so much fat and so many calories).

In addition, you need three tablespoons of some kind of fat every day. You might get it in the form of meat fat, mayonnaise, margarine, butter, or oil.

That's the ideal diet, but it's not the reality, as most of us know. The problem is that the effects of a poor diet aren't dramatic. Even if you ate nothing but bread and jam for two or three or four weeks (if you could stand it that long), your hair wouldn't fall out nor would your skin turn green. But your health would suffer in subtle ways. It may be years before the results of minimal nutrient deficiencies show up, or they may show up only as symptoms so mild that you blame them on studying too hard, or on working out too strenuously.

If you're a moderately active girl, you need between 2,100 and 2,400 calories a day just to maintain your weight. If you're a moderately active boy, you need between 2,600 and 3,000 calories a day. The *minimum* calorie level that can supply you with an adequate supply of nutrients is 1,500 to 1,800 calories a day—and that's only if you're eating food packed with nutrients and completely avoiding empty-calorie foods.

Most of the popular fad diets have many fewer than 1,500 calories—usually 500 to 800 calories a day. Such a diet is probably not dangerous if you follow it for only a week or two, but you'll regain the weight you lost very quickly once you go back to your normal eating pattern. If you're thinking of trying one of these diets, please talk to your doctor about it first. Some of them are better than others—and some can be dangerous.

If you're trying to lose weight, make sure you exercise more. Exercise not only helps you to burn more calories, it helps to regulate your body's metabolism so that you use calories more efficiently. Exercise will also protect you against losing muscle rather than fat when you take off weight. And, best of all, exercise does *not* increase your appetite, as you might expect; it actually seems to reduce it instead.

What are the best exercises? Anything you do consistently, every day. Walking, biking, roller-skating, jogging, swimming, and playing tennis are all fine. The point is that you have to expend more energy as well as eat fewer calories to lose weight effectively.

If you're seriously involved in competitive sports, you're probably not trying to lose weight. You probably need to eat *more* food to maintain your weight because of your greater energy expenditure. How much more you need depends on your size and the energy demands of the sport.

Many teenagers involved in athletics think that high-protein diets improve their performance, so they eat immense amounts of meat and milk. But the body's need for protein doesn't increase with exercise, the need for calories does, and these calories should come from all sources. Carbohydrates are probably the best thing to eat before an athletic competition. Coaches now recommend a balanced meal high in carbohydrates such as potatoes, bread, or spaghetti, followed by a few hours' rest, before the competition starts.

If you exercise strenuously, you'll lose a lot of body water and salt in the form of perspiration. You *must* replace what you lose. But drinks like Gatorade offer no advantage over plain water, and you don't need salt tablets to replace the salt —just salt your food or eat salted nuts, and drink plenty of water.

Your teen years are probably the first time you've had so much responsibility for choosing your own diet. When you pick out your own lunch in the school cafeteria or go to supper with your friends, it's your responsibility to choose an adequate amount and variety of food.

Though most teenagers eat sufficient amounts of the majority of nutrients, iron deficiency is common in the teen years. The body needs iron to insure proper muscle growth and to produce hemoglobin, the major part of red blood cells. About 75 percent of the teenagers in this country don't get enough iron in their diets—it's probably the most common deficiency for both boys and girls.

Iron deficiency will cause anemia if it's severe enough. Anemia is a condition in which the amount of hemoglobin (the protein that carries oxygen) in the blood is below normal. Symptoms of anemia include fatigue, loss of appetite, inability to concentrate, and irritability. Even if it doesn't cause anemia, lack of adequate iron in the diet can result in low energy levels and fatigue.

Meat is probably the best source of iron in the diet, but iron is absorbed more readily from any food if you eat something containing vitamin C at the same time—for example, a glass of orange juice along with a hamburger, or half a grapefruit at the same meal as scrambled eggs.

A vegetarian diet is the most likely to result in iron deficiency, because, by definition, a vegetarian diet excludes meat, poultry, and fish.

There are different kinds of vegetarians, and most don't eat *just* vegetables. Some vegetarians eat dairy products and eggs as well as fruits, nuts, and grains as well as vegetables. These vegetarians are known as ovolactovegetarians ("ovolacto" is "egg and milk" in Latin). Other vegetarians exclude eggs but still eat milk products; they're called lactovegetarians. Some go even further and eat *no* animal or dairy products at all, but only grains, fruits, vegetables, and nuts; these vegetarians are called vegans. The most rigorous vegetarian diet, and one that's dangerous to your health, is the Zen macrobiotic diet; in its most extreme form, it allows only cereal.

The basic fact about nutrition is this: the more kinds of food you eat, the easier it is to be well-nourished. As a vegetarian, you can eat a well-balanced selection of food that will keep you well-nourished *if* you're careful about your diet. Ovolactovegetarians can eat foods from all of the basic food groups, using eggs, beans, nuts, and seeds as substitutes for meat. The milk, cheese, and eggs in the diet supply calcium, iron, and other nutrients, and complement the vegetable proteins. Lactovegetarians can get these same nutrients from cheese and milk. But vegans are likely to suffer from deficiencies in several important vitamins and minerals, including vitamin B_{12}, vitamin D, calcium, and iron. The Zen macrobiotic diet should be avoided completely. If you follow a strict vegetarian diet, check with your doctor about taking a vitamin supplement.

Vegetarian or not, teenagers are often misled or confused when it comes to natural and organic foods. The terms "organic" food, "natural" food, and "health" food have somewhat different meanings. "Organic" food usually means food grown in soil on which no commercial pesticides were used. "Organic" meat comes from animals fed on "natural" feed, and not fed hormones or antibiotics. "Natural" foods are made from conventionally grown crops, but no additives or preservatives are put in the foods during processing. "Health" food is a more general term referring to all foods that are processed less than usual.

Claims made by natural-food producers can be misleading. So far, no scientific study has shown that organically grown crops are better for you nutritionally. And however they are grown, fresh fruits and vegetables that are shipped from distant places and stored for long periods of time lose some nutrients—whether they're stored in a health-food store or a supermarket.

Foods that you buy in a health-food store usually cost more, even if they're the same thing your local supermarket carries. Brand A from a supermarket = Brand A from a health-food store.

The best foods you can eat are those that have been processed the least, because more nutrients are removed during processing than are ever put back in. Whole-wheat bread is better for you than white bread, brown rice is more nutritious than white rice, and fresh or frozen orange juice is healthier than a drink made from orange-flavored crystals.

Most teenagers who are overweight or who don't want to gain any more weight consider anyone who has to add some pounds lucky indeed. But if you're thinner than you want to be, you know how difficult it is to gain weight.

If you are underweight, don't snack just before a meal if

it tends to spoil your appetite. Eat your snacks at least two hours before your meal. Try to put on some extra pounds by adding high-calorie snacks like peanut butter and crackers, granola, milk and cookies, and nuts. But don't go into a frenzy of eating candy and cupcakes because you'll be getting empty calories with not much nourishment.

If you add 500 calories a day to your diet, but keep your activity level the same, you should be able to gain a pound a week. Though you're underweight, don't stop regular exercise. Exercise is important for everyone, and will help you put on the extra pounds as muscle instead of flab.

The early teen years are a time when a lot of calories are expended in growth. As your growth rate slows down, you may start putting on weight.

One serious problem that's showing up more and more as teenagers become involved with dieting is anorexia nervosa, which is self-inflicted starvation.

At one time or another, everyone loses his or her appetite for a while—maybe because of a cold, or because it's just too hot to eat, or because of nervousness before an exam. That's normal appetite loss. But anorexia nervosa is loss of appetite that's of much longer duration and may lead to malnutrition and even death. It is abnormal behavior and results from psychological problems.

Once they start losing weight, anorexics don't stop. Because they can't see that they're becoming too thin, they eat less and less. They start to eat more and more slowly, and complain of feeling full after a bite or two.

Anorexics usually have several traits in common. They generally do well in school and are active in outside activities. Everyone thinks they're models of consideration and politeness. Typically, the eating disorder begins with a diet "just to take off a few pounds" so that "people will like me better."

Oddly enough, as they become emaciated, anorexics become more and more fascinated with food. They cook for others, collect recipes, and talk about food. Sometimes they do give in and eat a complete meal or go on an eating binge. But then they take laxatives or force themselves to vomit.

Though both boys and girls suffer from anorexia nervosa, girls are more likely to be anorexic than boys. An anorexic has a distorted picture of her body. She sees herself as either just right or still too fat even if she is fifty pounds underweight. This distorted body image usually began with a skewed idea of how fat she became when her body began to change during puberty. Very few anorexics really were too fat before they became anorexic.

The treatment of anorexia nervosa requires two separate approaches. First, the severe malnutrition must be corrected. Second, the psychological problems that caused the loss of appetite in the first place must be resolved. There is still some controversy about the best way to proceed, but anorexics are now usually hospitalized, and, while they are gaining weight in the hospital, they start some kind of family psychotherapy

ABOUT VITAMINS AND MINERALS

Vitamin	Function	Results of Deficiency	Natural Sources
A	Necessary for healthy eyes and skin. Helps to repair body tissue.	Difficulty seeing at night. Susceptibility to skin infections.	Green vegetables, carrots, sweet potatoes, dairy products.
B group	All vitamins in this group are necessary for the cells to function properly.		
B_1 (thiamine)	Needed for energy release and proper functioning of nervous system.	Beriberi, loss of appetite, fatigue.	Pork, beef, liver, whole grains.
B_2 (riboflavin)	Helps to control energy production and tissue building.	Swollen and cracked lips, blurred vision, red eyes, scaly skin rashes.	Milk, cheese, liver, fish, whole grains.
Niacin	Needed for energy release and normal growth.	Pellagra, weakness, scaly skin.	Meat, poultry, liver, fish, whole grains.
B_6	Necessary for growth. Essential for the nervous system.	Irritability, anemia.	Meat, vegetables, whole grains.
Pantothenic acid	Needed for growth and the production of antibodies.	Fatigue, muscle cramps.	Widely distributed in foods, especially whole grains, liver.

ABOUT VITAMINS AND MINERALS (cont.)

Vitamin	Function	Results of Deficiency	Natural Sources
B_{12}	Necessary for production of red blood cells and for growth.	Anemia, sore mouth and tongue.	Animal products only: liver, lean meat, dairy products.
Folic acid	Maintains healthy red blood cells.	Anemia.	Leafy green vegetables, whole grains.
C	Necessary to renew the "cement" that holds cells together. Important in healing.	Scurvy, bleeding gums, unexplained bruises, slow healing of wound.	Citrus fruits, strawberries, tomatoes.
D	Needed for bone and tooth development.	Rickets, weight loss, cramps, pain in bones.	Exposure to sunlight; fortified milk and margarine.
E (tocopherol)	Protects muscle tissue and red blood cells. Prevents cell damage.	Anemia.	Leafy green vegetables, wheat germ, vegetable oil, nuts.
K	Necessary for normal blood clotting.	Increased clotting time.	Leafy green vegetables; small amounts in other foods.

Minerals	Function	Results of Deficiency	Natural Resources
Calcium	Builds healthy teeth and bones. Helps to transmit nerve impulses.	Weak bones and teeth, impaired growth, muscle spasms.	Dairy products, dark green vegetables.
Phosphorus	Necessary for healthy bones and teeth. Helps to metabolize carbohydrates and fats	Weakness, poor growth.	Dairy products, meat, poultry, grains.
Potassium	Needed for nerve function and muscle contraction. Helps to control balance of water in the body.	Muscle weakness.	Milk, meat, bananas, oranges, and other fruits.
Sodium	Helps to control water balance and transmit nerve impulses.	Muscle cramps, reduced appetite.	Table salt, baking soda.
Magnesium	Essential for normal metabolism. Helps in normal muscle action.	Impaired growth.	Whole grains, leafy vegetables.
Iron	Essential for hemoglobin formation.	Anemia.	Liver, eggs, meat, whole grains.
Zinc	Enables the body to carry and release carbon dioxide. Neccessary for digestion. Helps in healing wounds.	Impaired growth, impaired sense of taste, poor appetite.	Widely distributed in foods, especially seafood, meat, whole grains, dairy products.

ABOUT VITAMINS AND MINERALS (cont.)

Minerals	Function	Results of Deficiency	Natural Sources
Copper	Necessary for production of red blood cells.	Anemia.	Oysters, liver, nuts and seeds.
Selenium	Works with vitamin E to help the body ward off disease.	Fragile red blood cells.	Garlic, seafood, meat.
Iodine	Important for proper functioning of thyroid gland.	Goiter(enlarged thyroid, impaired metabolism	Iodized table salt, seafood.
Chromium	Essential for energy .	Impaired glucose metabolism.	Liver, brewer's yeast.

combined with individual psychotherapy.

Anorexics often fail to see that they are responsible for what is happening to their bodies. They feel the anorexia is something that's happening to them, not something they are doing to themselves. If you have a friend who seems to be starving herself and you think it may be anorexia nervosa, don't think you're betraying her if you speak to her parents or to her doctor. Anorexics cannot stop starving themselves. In a case like this, you may save a life.

Bulimia, also called the "binge-purge syndrome," is another alarming eating disorder that's becoming more common. Bulimics go on eating binges, gorging uncontrollably on huge quantities of food and then try to purge themselves of the extra calories by vomiting or taking excessive amounts of laxatives.

Though it sounds as if this might be a good way to keep from gaining weight, it isn't. Because the stomach constantly empties its contents into the small intestine, a lot of the high-calorie binge food is digested and absorbed before it can be vomited or expelled by the use of laxatives. The medical complications (including heart rhythm abnormalities, fainting, and tooth decay) and psychiatric problems associated with bulimia are significant and dangerous.

Bulimics usually cannot break the habit without professional help. To find a therapist who specializes in eating disorders, call the department of psychiatry at a medical school or a mental health agency near you.

SKIN

Your skin is what you touch other people and things with, and where you, in turn, are touched by people and things, by sun and soap—and by poison ivy. Your skin protects the inside of your body, it helps to control your temperature, and it insulates you from cold and heat. It's where you meet the world—and that makes it as important to your appearance as it is to your health.

Your skin is more complicated than it looks. Seen through a microscope, even the smoothest skin looks like the surface of another planet, full of craters and ridges and valleys.

Skin has two layers. The outer layer is called the epidermis. It contains cells called keratinocytes and melanocytes. Keratinocytes produce the fibrin protein keratin, the principal constituent of the epidermis, hair, and nails. Melanocytes produce melanin, a pigment that gives your skin its color. Melanin absorbs ultraviolet light from the sun that would otherwise damage cells beneath the skin. When clusters of melanocytes become overactive in an attempt to protect the body from sun damage, freckles result. When melanocytes on all the exposed parts of your body protect you properly, you can see the result. It's called a suntan.

Everyone—black, white, or oriental—has the same number of melanocytes. Blacks, however, produce more melanin in each melanocyte than whites, and orientals produce an amount between the two.

The layer of skin under the epidermis is called the dermis. A great deal of the dermis is made up of collagen, a protein that gives skin its strength.

Dry skin is probably the most common wintertime complaint. Not only is outdoor air drier in winter than in summer, but indoor heating usually means that the air inside a house or school is dry. When air is heated but not humidified, the relative humidity (the amount of water in the air) goes down. As air becomes drier, moisture leaves the skin more quickly. If the skin's natural coating of oil is removed, the skin tends to lose even more moisture, and dry skin may become a problem. You should note, however, that having oily skin doesn't necessarily protect you against dry skin. Both conditions can occur simultaneously.

Soap and hot water are two things that remove oil and

contribute to dry skin. Though it's nice to be clean, you shouldn't be compulsive about washing, especially in the winter. Two or three showers or baths a day are too much for your skin. One shower or bath a day should be enough unless you have a tendency to dry skin, and then you may want to bathe even less frequently.

If your skin stays dry even when you bathe only once a day, try a bath oil in your tub. You can also use bath oil in the shower—pour a little into your hands and then rub it on your body just before you finally rinse off. You'll have to be careful about slipping in the shower or in the tub if you use bath oil; it's a good idea to use a rubber mat.

Use hand cream, body oil, or lubricating lotion while your skin is still moist. All of these work by trapping moisture under them so it can't evaporate; they do not add moisture themselves.

What kind of soap is best to use if your skin is dry? Any kind that doesn't irritate it. There's no advantage to one soap over another unless your skin is sensitive. If it is, try a very mild soap, like Dove or Neutrogena.

Deodorant soaps aren't any better than other soaps if you bathe or shower regularly and use an underarm deodorant or antiperspirant. In fact, they may irritate your skin. If you're using a deodorant soap and have itchy, red skin, switch to a mild, nondeodorant type.

No matter what soap you use or how careful you are about keeping your face clean, you'll probably have to contend with acne at some point. Almost everybody has some degree of acne during adolescence.

Though doctors don't know everything about the causes of acne, they do know a great deal. They know that the tendency to develop acne is probably inherited. And, while there's no complete cure yet, much has recently been learned about the nature of acne. Researchers have found that a great many things teenagers were urged to do in the past to prevent acne have no effect.

Diet, for example, plays no role either as a cause or cure for acne. There's really no evidence that eating chocolate, fatty foods, or spicy foods will trigger an acne flare-up. Occasionally someone will think he or she reacts to a specific food by breaking out in pimples, but this is the exception, not the rule. Of course, if your acne seems to get worse if you eat a specific food, it makes sense to cut it out of your diet.

Lack of cleanliness doesn't cause acne, either. Scrubbing your face two or three times a day with soap, hot water, and a washcloth and then using an astringent will probably only harm your skin by irritating and chapping it. You should keep your face clean, of course, but use a mild soap and warm water, be gentle, and use your hands rather than a washcloth.

Another myth that deserves to be forgotten is that masturbation or other sexual activity, too much sex or too little sex, or virginity will cause acne. Acne isn't influenced at all by sexual practices.

What does cause acne?

Everyone has oil glands—there are 15,000 to 20,000 in the face alone. At puberty, these oil glands start secreting more oil because of hormonal changes. Usually, the oil comes up a duct to the surface of the skin, where it can escape. Acne results when something goes wrong one-eighth of an inch below the skin's surface. The cells that line the duct and normally allow the oil to come to the surface freely seem to stick together and block the opening. As a result, oil gets trapped beneath the surface of the skin. When this happens, microscopic whiteheads form which may go on to rupture and cause pimples or may eventually become blackheads.

Blackheads are the mildest form of acne. Blackheads are mature whiteheads that gradually push their way to the skin's surface. Contrary to what most teenagers are told, they are not caused by dirt. The trapped oil looks black because bits of skin pigment (melanin) are caught in the oil. Blackheads are unsightly, but they rarely cause problems because they usually do not rupture and form pimples unless they are picked at.

The problems of acne are usually caused when the oil doesn't push its way to the surface as a blackhead but instead builds up and finally breaks through the wall of the oil gland. When this happens the oil inflames the skin around it and causes the redness, swelling, and pimples typical of acne.

Is there anything you can do for acne? Yes. Though there's no cure for acne yet, it can be controlled. Doctors have come a long way in learning how to treat it, so there's no need for anyone to suffer with acne for several years "because you'll outgrow it soon."

If you have an occasional small blemish or blackhead, the so-called "one-pimple acne" products you can buy in a drugstore without a prescription may be all you need. Look for acne lotions or creams that have sulfur, salicylic acid, or resorcinol in them. These cause your skin to peel, allowing the trapped oil to escape.

If your acne is somewhat worse, try a nonprescription (also called over-the-counter) product with benzoyl peroxide in it. Be careful to use it *exactly* the way the directions say to, because benzoyl peroxide can be irritating. If you apply a benzoyl peroxide lotion or cream too heavily, your skin can become red or inflamed. Use only a thin film. (Note: Some people are allergic to benzoyl peroxide.)

If you have a bad case of acne, make an appointment with a dermatologist (a doctor who specializes in the treatment of skin diseases). Today, dermatologists can get amazing results within three months in even the most stubborn cases of acne.

There is no single treatment for acne; dermatologists now use several treatments. After seeing you, your dermatologist will prescribe one of these for you.

Probably the most effective treatments for acne that a dermatologist can prescribe are those utilizing benzoyl peroxide, or vitamin-A acid, or (in more severe cases) a combination of the two. The vitamin-A acid breaks up the plugs blocking the oil ducts, and allows the oil to come to the surface. The benzoyl peroxide destroys bacteria in the whitehead and helps heal the pimples.

Dermatologists also use antibiotic creams and lotions to treat acne. These aren't the same as the antibiotic creams you buy to clear up infections, but are specially formulated mixtures available only by prescription.

For years, antibiotic pills were prescribed for stubborn cases of acne. There's nothing wrong with using pills, but anything that's taken internally might have side effects. With the new acne treatments doctors are now using, even severe forms of acne frequently can be controlled with creams and lotions applied to the skin rather than antibiotic pills. However, in some cases of acne, antibiotic pills may be necessary.

Anything that triggers the production of more oil will cause a flare-up of acne. When you're under stress or very anxious, for instance, your adrenal glands work overtime and stimulate the formation of hormones. These hormones, in turn, stimulate the production of oil. The normal cyclical fluctuation in hormone levels also explains why girls frequently have acne flare-ups just before a menstrual period. Perspiring heavily after exercise is associated with increased oil production; so is hot, humid weather, which appears to aggravate acne.

Many moisturizers, suntan lotions, and makeups contain

oil, and can contribute to your acne problem. If you use any of these products where acne usually occurs (chest, shoulders, back, face), make sure they're water-based—that is, oil-free.

Sometimes, even oil-free cosmetics can aggravate acne because they contain irritating chemicals. If you seem to break out after using an oil-free moisturizer, hair cream, or makeup, check with a dermatologist. He or she will be able to recommend a different brand. Hypoallergenic products— that is, those meant for people allergic to the usual ingredients in cosmetics—don't help in cases of acne, because acne starts *below* the surface of the skin and isn't caused by an allergy.

Sunlight seems to help some skin problems, including acne and oiliness, but these can be helped more by medicated products—and if you try a "sun cure," you may be trading a temporary improvement for permanent damage.

One of the ideas about a suntan that's been popular for a long time is that the tanner you are, the healthier you are. As far as your skin goes, the opposite is probably true. A suntan is your skin's way of protecting your body from the harm the sun can do.

We now know that radiation from sunlight damages the skin over time—and the effects start to build up the very first time you go out in the sun as a baby. Over the long run, the damage can include leathery, wrinkled skin and an increased

chance of skin cancer. Besides, sunlight triggers the formation of oil and whiteheads, and exposure to the sun may
actually result in acne flare-ups.

Does this mean you should never go into the sun again?
Of course not! But you have to be careful. The best thing you
can do for your skin is to use a sunscreen. Sunscreens protect
your skin by chemically absorbing the damaging part of the
sun's rays while allowing the tanning rays to get through. In
the radiation spectrum, the burning and tanning rays overlap, so you won't be able to get a tan without some damage
to your skin, but you can minimize the damage.

Most sunscreens on the market now have a sun-protection
factor (SPF) of anywhere from 2 to 15. The SPF tells you how
much longer you can stay in the sun without getting burned if
you use the sunscreen than if you don't. For instance, if you
can usually stay in the sun without any protection for half an
hour before you start to turn pink, a sunscreen with an SPF of
8 will protect you for four hours, a sunscreen with an SPF of 4
will protect you for two hours. Obviously, you have to know a
little bit about your own skin to employ a sunscreen intelli-
gently. A product with an SPF of 15 is valuable if you burn
easily or have a medical condition where you must avoid the
sun because such a product will block the burning and tanning rays completely.

Use a sunscreen whether you're fair or dark, and whether
you're tanned or not. The most effective sunscreens are those
containing para-aminobenzoic acid (PABA) and benzophe-

nones. (PABA absorbs the medium-length ultraviolet rays, and benzophenone compounds absorb the longer ultraviolet rays.) Put on sunscreen about thirty to forty-five minutes before you go into the sun, and check the label to see whether or not you have to reapply it at regular intervals after swimming.

Some other things to remember:

1. The sun is hardest on your skin between eleven in the morning and three in the afternoon. If you can stay out of the sun for those four hours, you'll save your skin from a lot of damage.

2. Even if the sun isn't shining, you can get a burn; ultraviolet rays can still come through on cloudy, hazy days.

3. A sun hat or beach umbrella won't protect you from burning, because sunlight will be reflected onto your face and body by sand and water. Use a sunscreen, especially if you're near the water or on a boat.

4. Contrary to popular belief, baby oil and iodine will not prevent a sunburn or encourage a tan. Use a regular sunscreen product that will protect your skin.

5. Lips can get sunburned, too. Use a colorless lip product meant to protect your lips from burning.

What if you do get a sunburn? The best way to relieve the pain is to soak in a tub of cool water. If only your face is burned, use a washcloth wrung out in plain, cool water. Hydrocortisone cream, now sold without a prescription, may also help. Be sure to use it only according to the directions.

Don't use any of the other preparations sold to relieve sunburn, because they often cause allergic skin reactions that make you feel even worse.

If you don't get an upset stomach from aspirin, two aspirin tablets every four hours when the burn is at its worst will help. Avoid prolonged use of aspirin, however, because this often has side effects.

Peeling always follows a severe sunburn, and there's nothing that will prevent it from happening. Baby oil or moisturizer will make your skin feel less rough, but won't stop the peeling.

If you want to look suntanned without going into the sun, chemical tanning preparations are safe to use if you're not sensitive or allergic to the ingredients. They do not actually tan you, but stain the skin. Stay away from them if you break out in a rash or feel as if your skin is burning when you use them.

"Bronzers" also contain a pigment that stains the skin. Again, they're safe to use if you're not allergic or sensitive to the ingredients.

Chemical tans and bronzers *do not* protect the skin from sunburn unless they contain a sunscreen. Read the label!

Ultraviolet lamps and suntanning booths are two ways of getting a tan that should be completely avoided. A lot of people think they're safer than sunlight. They're not. If you can't stay in the sun without burning, you can't get a tan from an ultraviolet lamp or in a booth, either. And then, people who use suntanning booths may be exposed to *twice* the cancer-producing ultraviolet radiation than natural sunlight delivers. Radiation meters used in these booths can be inaccurate and can seriously underestimate exposure.

Many doctors are also concerned about possible damage to the eyes from ultraviolet lamps and suntanning booths. This is one way of getting a tan that's more damaging than fun. The risks aren't worth it.

Your skin is prone to several rashes that can look frightening but usually don't cause any lasting damage. Among them are jock itch, prickly heat, pityriasis rosea, and contact dermatitis.

Jock itch is the common term for fungus infections affecting the groin. All of them are made worse by heat and moisture. Boys who are physically active and perspire heavily are most likely to be affected. Sometimes the rash is caused by the same fungus that causes athlete's foot and the infection may spread from the feet to the groin. Jock itch can also be caused by chafing or irritation by underpants or a jock strap. If the rash appeared just after you started wearing new underpants or a new jock strap, that may be the cause. A switch to loose cotton underwear (not nylon or polyester) may help. Use a non-irritating powder to keep the area dry. If the rash doesn't clear in a week or two, see a doctor about it.

If sweat remains in the ducts of the sweat glands instead of coming to the surface of the skin where it can evaporate, an inflamed, tiny red bump appears. These bumps are called prickly heat. The rash most often comes on in hot, humid weather, but it can also be caused by a high fever or by heavy winter clothing that doesn't allow sweat to evaporate. Prickly heat will clear up by itself in a few days. If it itches, a cool bath is soothing.

Pityriasis rosea (PR) is a common, completely harmless rash that usually shows up as scaly patches. One large spot precedes the rest of the breakout. This spot is called a "herald patch" because it heralds the arrival, in five to ten days, of the rest of the rash. Typically, the patches form a Christmas-tree pattern on the back. The rash lasts anywhere from two to twelve weeks (usually about six weeks), and disappears by itself. Cool baths or showers and calamine lotion will help to ease the itching.

Contact dermatitis is the technical name for a rash caused by a "contact"-type allergic reaction. Cells on the skin react by becoming inflamed *only* at the place where the allergy-causing substance (allergen) has touched you. Poison ivy is the most common form of contact dermatitis, but almost anything that touches your skin can cause a reaction if you're sensitive to it. For example, costume jewelry often causes an allergic reaction because of the nickel content of the metal. (To test yourself for nickel sensitivity, scrape an old five-cent piece and hold it in place against the skin of your arm with a Band-Aid for twenty-four hours. If you're sensitive to nickel, there'll be a red splotch on your skin.)

Sometimes cosmetics or sunscreens won't cause a rash by themselves, but will cause an exaggerated reaction to sunlight. Your skin will become red, puffy, and itchy wherever you've used the sunscreen or cosmetic. If the reaction is to lipstick or lip pomade, your lips may become chapped even in the summer.

Obviously, to prevent contact dermatitis you must avoid whatever causes it. If you're sensitive to nickel and still want to wear costume jewelry, coat it with clear nail polish before you wear it. (Stainless steel won't cause any problems.) If you do get a rash and it's weepy and itches, use cool-water compresses or cool-water baths several times a day to soothe the skin. You can also try the hydrocortisone creams sold to control itching. Do *not* use them on cold sores or in the eyes. If they don't help, see your doctor.

Some skin disorders are caused by living creatures. One of them, scabies, is a very itchy condition caused by a mite so tiny that the adult female looks like a speck of dust. The male is half that size. Both the male and female burrow into the skin and lodge just below the surface. The female lays eggs that hatch in three or four days, and the new mites keep the infestation going.

The worst thing about scabies is the itching, which is often intolerable at night. The scabies mite prefers to lodge between the fingers, at the wrists, elbows, and ankles, and in the groin.

Scabies is most often spread through intimate contact with an infected person, but people can also get a certain type of scabies from a dog or cat if the animal is infected and if it is picked up, petted, or held close.

The treatment for scabies is simple and painless—a lotion or cream is applied to the skin for several days. But neither the lotion nor the cream is available without a prescription, so see your doctor if you think you have scabies.

There are three kinds of lice that bother people—head lice, body lice, and pubic lice (also called "crabs"). Though each kind looks a little different from the others and prefers a different part of the body, all three cause itching. If you have any kind of lice, the condition is known medically as pediculosis.

Body and head lice are related and look somewhat alike; pubic lice look like crabs (hence their nickname). Female lice live for about a month and lay up to ten eggs a day. The eggs hatch in about a week and take another week to mature.

Head lice usually remain on the scalp, but can also infest beards, eyelashes, and eyebrows. They cause severe itching. Although the lice themselves are hard to see, their eggs (or "nits") can be seen sticking to hairs. Nits look like dandruff, but can't be brushed off. You can catch head lice by using someone else's comb, brush, clothing, eye makeup, football helmet, or hat. They're *very* contagious.

Body lice are transmitted by clothing or bedding. They don't live on the skin—they go there only for meals.

"Crab" lice live mainly in pubic hair, but can also be found in body and armpit hair and on eyelashes. Crabs are usually spread by sexual contact, but you can also catch them from infested bedding.

Treatment for lice is simple. A liquid medication applied to the skin is available without a prescription and frequently will do the job. If it doesn't, see your doctor, who will give you a prescription for a different medication.

Two common skin conditions are caused by viruses. These are cold sores and warts.

"Cold sores" are an infection caused by a virus that enters the body through a small break in the skin. The first time the virus enters the body, the infection (usually herpes simplex) may or may not cause symptoms and you may not know you have any infection.

After the infection clears up, the virus remains in the nerve near the place where it caused the original infection. Then, whenever your body is under physical or emotional stress, the virus will have a chance to overcome your body's defenses and cause outbreaks of blisters.

No one can catch the herpes virus from you if you don't have blisters. If you do have them, the virus is very contagious until the blisters dry completely.

There aren't any medicines that will rid your body of the herpes virus. If you do get cold sores, you can try patting them with rubbing alcohol or salt water every couple of hours to speed up the drying. If they persist, and particularly if they're in or around the eyes, see your doctor.

Whether you get warts or not depends on whether your body can fight the virus infection that causes them. Warts are *not* caused by handling toads and are not "catching" in the same way that measles and mumps are.

If your body isn't resistant to the wart virus, any irritation or small cut or scrape in the skin may help the virus to enter. Once in, it will multiply and cause your skin cells to grow too much, forming a bump, or wart. It takes anywhere from a few weeks to several months after the virus enters the skin for a wart to form.

Warts are annoying, but they're harmless. If you've got only one or two and they don't bother you, try to ignore them. They will probably disappear without any treatment within a year or two. If you want to speed up the process, try any wart remedy you can buy in a drugstore. Use it *only* according to directions, and wait at least a month to see if it works.

Doctors use several methods to treat warts, including dissolving, cauterizing or freezing them. If you go to a doctor, don't expect him or her to get rid of a wart in just one treatment. Some very small warts will disappear this quickly, but most won't. And remember, since warts are caused by a virus, they may recur.

Finally, there are hypnotism, self-hypnotism, and suggestion, which seem to work with some people and not with others. If someone is convinced that a gold ring rubbed on a wart will make it disappear, such a treatment may indeed work. Or, if a doctor tells a patient to come back in three weeks to have the wart removed surgically, it may disappear within those three weeks. No one knows why this works, or even why it works with some people and not with others.

HAIR

No part of you grows faster than your hair (which will keep growing longer even when you stop growing taller), yet hair itself is dead. Because it is made by live body cells, however, the state of health of your hair reflects the health of your body.

Though a strand of hair looks like a simple thread, it's really a complicated structure. Each hair consists of a shaft (the part you see) and a root that's embedded in a hair follicle. Follicles are the small pockets that produce hair; they are buried in the skin. Everyone has about 100,000 follicles on the scalp alone. (Follicles never die, but many eventually cease to produce long, thick hairs—which accounts for bald heads.)

Each hair has three layers. The outside layer, the cuticle, is made up of fine, flattened scales of protein that overlap one another to form a protective, flexible armor. (Under a microscope, the cuticle looks much like a tightly closed pine cone.) Though you can't see the scales with the naked eye, you can feel them. Take a single hair and run your fingers down it, starting at the scalp. The hair feels smooth because you're flattening the scales in the direction they lie. If you run your fingers from the end of the hair toward your scalp, you'll feel a slight roughness—you are rubbing the scales against the grain.

The middle layer, the cortex, makes up the bulk of each hair. The cortex consists of ribbons of protein that twist around each other and give hair its strength and elasticity. The cortex also contains pigments that give hair its natural color.

A central column, the medulla, runs through the cortex. Scientists aren't certain about the function of the medulla, but they believe it's necessary for the proper growth of hair.

Each hair on your head does *not* constantly grow longer. There is a natural cycle that governs the growth of hair. Each hair root is always in one of three stages: growing, transition, or resting. The growing phase of each hair lasts, on the average, three years. During that time, the hair grows one-quarter to one-half an inch a month. Then the root goes into a transition phase that lasts about two weeks, and finally into a resting phase that lasts for three or four months. At the end of this time, the matrix (the active growing area) enters the growing phase again, and the resting hair is pushed out from below by a new growing hair. Normally, we lose fifty to 150 hairs every day.

Fortunately, scalp hairs are not all in the same phase of this cycle at the same time. If they were, we would periodically shed all our hair. At any one time, about 80 to 90 percent of the hair is growing, 5 percent is in the transition phase, and the remainder is in the resting stage. Hairs that are resting stay in place for a few months before they're pushed out.

Though the average growing phase lasts about three years, some people have hair with a growing phase of as long as six years. Because hair grows at the same rate on all of us, this difference in the length of the growing phase explains why some girls can grow very long hair while others simply cannot, no matter how hard they try. Cutting or not cutting your hair won't speed up the rate at which it will grow, nor will it "strengthen" it.

Your general state of health affects the way your hair looks and grows. Constant dieting, severe illness, and certain drugs can all change your body's metabolism enough to slow down the rate of growth and cause thinner, more brittle hair to grow. These hairs break easily and don't have the shine and luster of healthy hair.

If you've been ill, normal hair will usually start to grow again when you are over the illness. But if you've been dieting severely, you'll have to add protein-rich foods (such as milk, meat, and eggs) to your diet if you want your hair to start looking healthy.

To keep your hair looking its best, you must shampoo it, of course. But no matter what the advertisements say, all shampoos work the same way: a group of chemicals called alkalis trap the dirt and grease that are on the hair so that they can be washed away. These alkalis also relax the protein scales of the hair cuticle so that they fan open and the dirt trapped underneath can be rinsed away. All soaps and detergents contain alkalis, and all work exactly the same way, so you could just as well use hand soap or dishwashing liquid to shampoo your hair—and some people do. The best shampoo for your hair is the one that you like best. It's as simple as that.

There's no need to suds your hair more than once at each shampooing, no matter what the directions say. Unless your hair is very dirty, sudsing more than once only strips away necessary oil and dries out your hair.

Because hair itself is dead, no shampoo can give you "healthier" hair, despite what the commercials and advertisements claim. Shampoo is washed out of your hair when you rinse, and along with it go any eggs, protein, and fruit oil that are in it. Healthy hair is the result of a healthy person and a healthy diet. Nothing you put on your hair in the way of shampoos can change that fact.

Many teenagers like to use a conditioner after shampooing, and that's fine—but don't expect miracles from them.

There's no conditioner that will mend, repair, or permanently alter your hair. What conditioners do is temporarily fill in any chips or cracks on the hair shaft so that it feels smoother. They also "glue" split ends together until the next shampoo washes your hair clean again, and they coat your hair so that it feels thicker.

Conditioners are fine for your hair if you don't overuse them. If you use a conditioner and a conditioning shampoo, your hair will start looking greasy: it's being overconditioned. You can also overcondition your hair if you use a conditioner every time you shampoo. If your hair seems limp and has no body no matter what shampoo and conditioner you use, try using shampoo alone for two or three washings. Then, if you start to use conditioner again, use it only every third washing.

Though conditioners will temporarily glue together split ends, they won't cure them. Split ends are not the end of the world, but they are something you should pay attention to. Very long hair will split at the ends if it's not trimmed regularly. Hair that's overtreated (blown dry too often, twisted tightly on hard rollers or curlers, and so forth) will split at the ends from being abused.

Because hair is dead tissue, it doesn't hurt when you mistreat it, but it does let you know that something's wrong. And split ends are one way your hair tells you you're being too harsh on it.

The only way to get rid of split ends is to cut them off.

Conditioners are only a temporary remedy; there's no way to glue split ends together permanently.

You can avoid getting split ends in the first place by easing up on what you do to your hair. Use a natural-bristle brush rather than a nylon brush. Don't use the high heat setting on your hot-air dryer—use medium heat. And don't overdry your hair—leave some moisture in it when you're finished. Don't use a hair dryer every time you shampoo. If your hairstyle holds its shape only if it's dried with a hair dryer, it's time to get a different style. Overusing hair dryers is one of the commonest causes of split ends and dry scalp. If you use rollers, use foam rollers instead of brush rollers; foam is gentler on your hair.

What about dandruff? Anyone can have dandruff. You can have it whether your hair is oily, normal, or dry, and there is no permanent cure. Dandruff is not a disease, it is merely an annoying condition.

The skin all over your body replaces itself constantly. New cells are formed and old cells are shed. The skin on your scalp does the same thing—but if the cells are shed as clumps instead of microscopic single cells, you have dandruff. Why this happens to some people and not to others is still a mystery. But we do know that dandruff is not caused by a germ and is not "catching."

You can usually control dandruff by using an antidandruff shampoo once a week. Antidandruff shampoos are drying, so, if you wash your hair oftener than once a week, you will probably want to use a regular dry-hair shampoo in between treatments with the dandruff shampoo. A conditioner may be helpful.

Sometimes very dry scalps will shed flakes of dead skin cells. If this is the problem, using an antidandruff shampoo will dry out the scalp even more, causing more flaking.

How do you tell the difference between dandruff caused by dry scalp and other dandruff? Use a dry-hair shampoo and conditioner two or three times. If your problem is dry scalp, the scaling should slow down and become less noticeable. If it does, continue with dry-hair shampoos and forget about antidandruff shampoos.

If neither antidandruff shampoo nor dry-hair shampoo works and your dandruff remains severe, and if you have itching and redness of the scalp, you may have a condition known as seborrhea or seborrheic dermatitis. It's not dangerous, it's not catching, and it can be treated effectively with special shampoos. But they're available only by prescription, so you should see your doctor.

Hair spray won't cause dandruff, but sprays coat the hair to keep it in place, and when you brush your hair after using a spray, the coating will break up into small particles that flake off and look like dandruff. Leaving soap around your hairline when you wash your face won't cause dandruff, either, but the bits of soap that dry on your skin will look like dandruff when you brush them off.

TEETH

Your smile is one of the first things people notice about you, so keeping your teeth healthy and sparkling and your mouth in good condition will pay dividends.

By the time you're twelve or thirteen, you should have all of your adult teeth except the four wisdom teeth that will come in when you're about eighteen. These teeth have to last you for the rest of your life—and there are things you can start doing now to make sure they remain in good condition.

Your teeth's worst enemies are the bacteria that live in your mouth. These bacteria glue themselves to your teeth by forming a furry film called plaque. Plaque is the invisible villain that causes both cavities and gum disease.

Every time you eat food containing sugar, the bacteria in

your mouth break down that sugar and produce an acid that begins to destroy your teeth. This "acid attack" on the tooth's surface lasts for at least an hour, so frequent snacks of cake, sticky candy, and soft drinks will mean your teeth are under an almost continuous acid attack.

Though you'll often hear people say that "cavities run in the family," there's little scientific evidence to support this claim. Children often have the same eating habits and tooth-cleaning habits as their parents, however—and these two sets of habits heavily influence the formation of caries, which is what professionals call the disease that causes cavities.

Caries is not simply a matter of chance. There are three things involved in the decay of teeth: bacteria in plaque, sugar-rich foods, and natural resistance to caries. Teenagers vary in their resistance to caries; one may be totally caries-free while another has rampant caries. (Dentists define rampant caries as more than five new cavities in one year.)

One fact that's little known is that teeth eventually build up a resistance to caries. Teeth are most susceptible to decay for three to four years after they come in—generally when you're between twelve and sixteen years old. During this time, the teeth gradually absorb fluoride and other substances from saliva that make them less prone to decay. If you can escape new cavities during this critical period, your chances of avoiding them completely will improve considerably.

Plaque will grow on your teeth as a matter of course. If you don't remove it from the gum line after twenty-four hours, the bacteria in it will cause a chronic gum infection that can go on to destroy the bone that supports the teeth. This infection is called gingivitis in its early stages, and periodontal disease when it begins to destroy bone.

You may notice that your gums bleed slightly when you brush your teeth. That's one of the first signs of gingivitis. But sometimes the bleeding is so slight that you don't notice it yourself. That's one reason to make regular appointments with your dentist. If gingivitis is allowed to progress, the teeth become loose, and they may eventually fall out. It is usually periodontal disease that makes it necessary for people to replace their natural teeth with false teeth.

There's good evidence that removing plaque thoroughly will prevent gingivitis and help to prevent caries. If you haven't been visiting a dentist or dental hygienist for professional cleanings, you should start now. Professional cleaning doesn't hurt, and it does start you off properly on your own cleaning routine. Your dentist or dental hygienist will also be glad to show you the proper way to clean your teeth at home.

To control plaque, you need to do more than just brush your teeth. First of all, use dental floss. Some people think that floss is needed only to remove bits of food stuck between the teeth. It's important to remember that the real purpose of flossing is to remove plaque—and that flossing reaches plaque located where gum infection is most likely to develop. Establish a routine time for flossing: before you go to bed, when you watch television, or when you're reading. But make sure you make it a routine and floss once every day.

How do you floss correctly? Break off a piece of floss about fifteen inches long and wind one end around the index finger of one hand, the other end around the index finger of the other hand. Use your thumbs to guide a short length between two teeth. Slide the floss up or down to the gum line—gently —and move it back and forth or up and down against the sides of the teeth. Repeat this on all the rest of your teeth.

The next time you see your dentist, ask him or her to check your flossing technique with a special plaque stain. The stain shows exactly how well you're cleaning your teeth—and where you aren't cleaning well enough. To learn to clean your teeth properly may take several practice sessions under the supervision of your dentist or dental hygienist.

Brushing probably isn't as all-important as you've been told, but it's still something that should become a twice-a-day routine. When you brush your teeth, hold the toothbrush with the bristles at right angles to your teeth, and brush from side to side along the gum line with short strokes. Brush the inner and outer surfaces of both the upper and lower teeth, and finish up by brushing the chewing surfaces. Whether your water is fluoridated or not, use a fluoridated toothpaste approved by the American Dental Association. (Look on the toothpaste tube for a small shield that says "Accepted, Council on Dental Therapeutics, American Dental Association.")

Most dentists now recommend a brush with soft bristles that have rounded tips and a flat brushing surface. This kind of brush is least likely to damage your teeth and gums. A brush that has missing or bent bristles won't do much good, so check your brush often and plan to invest in a new one three or four times a year. A worn brush won't remove plaque effectively no matter how often you use it.

When you rinse your mouth after brushing, squirt the water between your cheeks and tongue to dislodge any food particles stuck between the teeth. If you want to use a mouth-wash, too, go ahead, but don't expect it to kill many germs in your mouth or guarantee fresh breath.

If your teeth are stained, brush them more often, but don't use a polishing toothpaste that claims to remove stains from teeth. Such a toothpaste will wear away the hard enamel of the teeth and create sensitive, unsightly grooves where your teeth meet your gums. If you can't control the staining at home, have your teeth cleaned more often by a dentist or dental hygienist. Incidentally, healthy teeth are not necessarily very white. A very attractive normal color varies from slightly yellow to slightly gray.

You should clean your teeth at least twice a day—once in the morning and once at night. Better yet, brush immediately after you eat, and especially after you eat a sugar-rich snack food. Even if that's not always possible, it's usually possible to get a drink of water. First swish the water around in your mouth; then swallow it. It's not a perfect way to clean your teeth, but it is unobtrusive and better than letting small bits of food remain in your mouth.

For the sake of your teeth and gums, as well as for your general health, it's important to eat a well-balanced diet. Of specific help for your teeth and gums is limiting your intake of sugar-rich foods. There very definitely is a relationship between sugar and caries. How often you eat sugar-rich foods directly influences tooth decay. Repeatedly eating sugar-rich snack foods will keep the bacteria in plaque busy producing the acid that destroys your teeth.

Sugar in a liquid (like soft drinks) isn't as bad for your teeth as sugar in sticky foods like jelly beans and caramels, because it doesn't remain in your mouth as long. Fresh fruit is a healthier snack than candy, but the sugar in fruit (yes, even in apples) will also damage your teeth if it's not removed, so brush or rinse your mouth even after snacks of fruit. For the sake of your teeth, if you're going to chew gum, make sure it's sugarless gum.

Many advertisements and radio and television commercials aimed at teenagers warn of the danger of bad breath, and everyone has had some experience with someone whose breath isn't as fresh as it should be.

What causes bad breath? Bad breath can be caused by several things: plaque buildup, decayed teeth, a nose or throat infection, or gum disease. Mouthwash won't correct the cause of bad breath, and will mask the odor only for a short while. The only cure for bad breath is to find the cause and correct it.

If you think you have bad breath, start out by brushing and flossing your teeth twice a day without fail, and either brushing or rinsing your mouth every time you finish eating, whether it's a cookie or a whole meal. If the cause of the bad breath is plaque buildup or decaying food that's been allowed to remain in your mouth, this should solve the problem. If your bad breath remains, pay a visit to your dentist, because you may have caries or gum disease. If this is what's causing the odor, you'll require professional help.

Bad breath after eating garlic or onions is not caused just by the odor lingering in your mouth. When you digest these foods, certain by-products are formed; these circulate in your bloodstream and are given off by your lungs. If you want to prove this to yourself, swallow a small clove of garlic whole, clean your teeth, and check your breath an hour later. In spite of these precautions, you'll still smell of garlic.

If you're unhappy with the way your teeth look, or if you have trouble chewing or biting, you may want to see an orthodontist about getting braces. Orthodontists (dentists who specialize in straightening teeth) are now using new kinds of braces that have more clear plastic and less metal in them than the older kinds. They're not invisible, but they're a lot less noticeable than the old "railroad tracks."

If you need braces, you will have to wear them for anywhere from six months to four years—the length of time will depend on the kind of problem that you have. If you do wear braces, be extra careful to avoid sugar and to clean your teeth carefully, because your teeth are more prone to caries and gingivitis than if you didn't wear braces. You should also use a special fluoride mouth rinse every day to strengthen your teeth against caries.

You probably don't expect to fall and knock out a tooth, or to have one knocked out during a sports activity—but it can happen. If you lose a tooth—roots and all—rinse it off, put it in a container, cover it with water, and take it to the nearest dentist. Chances are that it can be replaced in its socket and will heal into place. The important thing to remember is that the tooth should not dry out. If there's no water available, put the tooth under your tongue to keep it moist.

If you chip off just part of your tooth, there's no way to reattach it. Some people have tried using epoxy glue, but it doesn't work. Make an appointment immediately to have your dentist check the tooth. He or she can probably restore the missing part with a new material that fuses to the tooth.

Another troublesome condition that can affect your mouth is a canker sore. Canker sores are painful sores that occur on the inside of the mouth and last anywhere from seven to fourteen days. They heal up by themselves, and rarely leave scars.

No one knows exactly what causes canker sores. There seems to be some relationship between canker sores and stress, and the tendency to develop them is inherited. There is no successful treatment for canker sores yet, though some doctors and dentists do prescribe a special mouth rinse to reduce the pain. If you get canker sores and they aren't too painful, try to ignore them; remember, they'll go away by themselves. But if you are bothered by frequent, painful canker sores, see your dentist. He or she can prescribe something to make you more comfortable.

Your teenage years are the time to start taking advantage of what modern dentistry has to offer. A lot has changed since the days when your grandmother attached one end of a string to her tooth and the other end to a doorknob so she could pull the tooth out herself and avoid a visit to the dentist. Dentists today are more interested in preventing caries and gum disease than in treating them. Too many adults have to go for treatment because of problems that started when they were your age. You can sail through these critical years if you make regular appointments to see your dentist, limit your between-meal snacks of sugar-rich foods, and clean your teeth thoroughly and regularly.

SLEEP

As a child, you probably said, "But I want to stay up longer!" Sleep seemed such a terrible waste of time when there was so much to do. Going to bed excluded you from the exciting, grown-up, evening-hours world that your older brothers and sisters and the adults around you were privileged to participate in. Struggling over bedtime is a standard feature of childhood.

By now, though, you have more control over when you go to bed and how long you sleep. Statements about not wanting to go to bed are likely to change to questions such as, "Am I getting enough sleep?" or "Am I getting too much sleep?" or "Why do I have trouble falling asleep?"

Just why do we sleep? We don't understand the role of sleep completely yet, but it seems that all of us need to sleep to restore both the body and the mind. It also seems that we need to sleep because we need to dream.

An average night's sleep follows a pattern. There are five stages of sleep; four of them are repeated several times a night. Each stage can be identified by its own distinct brain-wave pattern as measured on an electroencephalograph (EEG), an instrument that records electrical activity in the brain.

Stage 1, the lightest stage of sleep, is that time when you've first fallen asleep and can be wakened easily. This stage occurs just once, unless you wake up completely and then go back to sleep. Some scientists feel that stage 1 sleep is so light it hardly should be considered sleep.

After a few minutes, you enter stage 2 sleep, which, as you'd imagine, is somewhat deeper. After a few minutes more you drift into stage 3, and, within half an hour to an hour, you're in stage 4 sleep, the deepest sleep of all, and the hardest to wake from. (It's during stage 4 sleep that people walk in their sleep.)

During stage 4 sleep, your heart rate slows considerably and your brain waves show a slow, regular rhythm. It's at this stage of sleep that you sweat more, because the part of the brain that controls sweating is no longer operating. You also move and turn more—up to fifty times a night. If you're wakened from stage 4 sleep by the telephone or by an alarm, you feel confused and have to take a moment to start thinking straight again.

From stage 4 sleep, you enter what's called rapid-eye-movement (REM) sleep—the stage at which you dream. During REM sleep your body hardly moves, but your brain becomes suddenly active, and the amount of blood going to it increases. You move your eyes rapidly beneath your closed eyelids as you watch the Technicolor motion pictures your brain projects for you—your dreams.

From REM sleep, you drift back to stage 2 again, then stages 3 and 4, and once again enter REM sleep. There are four or five of these cycles each night; one begins about every ninety minutes. Dreams (REM sleep) take up about 20 percent of the time you sleep during the teen years—more than during adulthood.

Everyone needs REM sleep. Experiments have been conducted in which people were allowed to sleep, but were denied dream time (they were wakened when they started to dream). The subjects in these experiments became anxious and irritable, and had trouble concentrating during the day. When they were then allowed both to sleep and dream, they dreamed about 50 percent more than usual for several nights. The body and mind must have dreaming sleep to function, because dreaming is important to learning. We need REM sleep to understand new information and to keep us in emotional balance. Even if you can't remember dreams from the night before, you have had several periods of REM sleep if it was an average night.

Dreams last anywhere from five to forty minutes, depending on whether they come at the beginning or end of a night's sleep. Dreams at the start of a night's sleep are shorter than those at the end. Though dreams seem to flash by when you're dreaming them, the things that happen in them take the same amount of time to dream as they would take to happen in real life. Dreams take place in color, but we often don't remember the colors, just as we often don't remember colors in real-life events. We're more concerned with what's happening than with the colors.

Sometimes rather strange things happen in dreams, and you may find the contents of your dreams puzzling or upsetting. Dreams aren't mysterious, however, and the ones we remember may have a connection to something that's happened to us. We know that things that happen during the day don't *start* us dreaming, but daily happenings can affect what happens in a dream. It's fun to trace back a remembered dream to see if anything that happened the day before affected it in some way. For instance, if your geography assignment is to figure out what time it is in Japan when it's ten in the morning here, you might dream about piloting a plane across the ocean.

Dreams do have an "inner meaning," but to get at the inner meaning of a dream you must unravel it on the basis of *your* experiences and *your* thoughts. Some symbols or situations that commonly appear in dreams do tend to have the same general meaning to everybody, but their exact meaning for you has to relate to your own life.

Dreams are often said to represent or fulfill the dreamer's wishes. But a dream can have many different meanings to you, so don't think that what seems to happen in your dream is *really* what you wish. Your dream can mean you really wish that, or that you really wish just the opposite—or that you really wish something that didn't appear to happen in the dream at all. It takes a great deal of skill to help someone unravel the meaning of a dream. No one with professional experience working with people's dreams would ever say that he or she could give an exact interpretation of your dream from what you tell about it, because a dream can have so many meanings. Dream books and newspaper columns that interpret dreams are fun to read, but don't take them too seriously.

Each of the five stages of sleep is necessary. It's now believed that stages 1 through 4 allow the body to repair itself physically, while REM sleep allows the brain to repair itself and to form new connections that permit us to continue thinking and learning.

Our sleep waking cycles are part of what's called the body's circadian cycle or biologic rhythm. In everyday life, internal clocks are set to a day of approximately twenty-four hours. (If we are on vacation and don't have to stay on a schedule, we will usually wake up a bit later than usual and go to sleep a bit later each day.) Body-temperature rhythms usually are coordinated with sleep rhythms so that we sleep at the time when our body temperature is lowest and we're the most vulnerable physically.

How much sleep do you really need? The answer has a lot to do with your age, but the specific number of hours is difficult to specify precisely. The number of hours people sleep changes as they grow older. Infants sleep from twelve to sixteen hours each day. By the age of five, children usually stop napping and average eleven hours of sleep each night. Teenagers need more sleep than adults—usually between eight and ten hours a night—but there is no absolute number of hours that's considered "correct." Teenagers usually have difficulty waking up, but if you go through the day without feeling tired once you are awake, you're getting enough sleep. If you're not sleeping enough, you will feel tired and droopy-eyed all day.

Everyone needs sleep, but not getting a good night's sleep for one or two nights won't hurt you. Your attention span and reaction time won't be as good as usual, but the most harmful thing about not getting enough sleep for a few nights is usually the worry about not having slept.

Sleeping patterns can be disturbed by any number of things. Problems with school or family, nervousness about an upcoming exam or party, illness, drug use, or an uncomfortable bed are a few of the things that can disrupt a night's sleep.

It seems to be not only the amount of sleep you get that's important, but also, the proportion of REM sleep to non-REM sleep that you get. It's also important that you have a fairly regular sleep schedule. An irregular schedule with sudden shifts in sleep and waking times can affect your alertness and performance. If you constantly change your sleep schedule, you may feel logy even if you've slept the same number of hours each night.

Both sleeping pills and alcohol (in beer, wine, and hard liquor) can cause more problems with sleep than they solve. Any sedative drug allows you to go to sleep more easily for a while, but prevents you from going through the normal stages of sleep. Alcohol and sleeping pills produce something like light anesthesia and drastically reduce the amount of REM sleep you get. If you're using either one every night, going to sleep will eventually become harder and harder for you. Once you stop using sleeping pills or alcohol, it will take a while for your body to readjust, and your sleep will be disturbed until it does.

Other substances that can affect sleep are stimulants, hallucinogens, tobacco, and caffeine. Stimulant drugs ("uppers") interfere with going to sleep and staying asleep whether you use them once in a while or often. Hallucinogenic drugs can make the period just before going to sleep very frightening. Cigarettes and caffeine both stimulate the nervous system and make falling asleep difficult.

Certain physical problems can also be responsible for abnormal sleep patterns. For instance, the first symptom of infectious mononucleosis may be sleepiness. Both asthma and menstrual irregularities may cause sleep problems.

Two illnesses directly involving sleep sometimes appear during the teen years. One of them is narcolepsy, characterized by unpredictable attacks of sleep during the day. Other symptoms of narcolepsy include feeling unable to move just before going to sleep at night or just after waking in the morning; brief attacks of muscle weakness after laughing or getting angry; and peculiar or frightening hallucinations before falling asleep at night. Narcolepsy is a physical disease that can be treated. (Note: Though many teenagers complain of constant sleepiness during the day, it's usually not narcolepsy. If you're sleepy during the day, try getting more sleep at night. You don't need to be too worried about yourself unless the other symptoms of narcolepsy are also present.)

Sleep apnea is another physical illness; it's caused by a blockage in the respiratory tract. A person with sleep apnea wakes up constantly during the night gasping for breath. Because nighttime sleep is disturbed, the victim of sleep apnea is tired during the day, and often has headaches and periods when he or she does tasks routinely but doesn't remember doing them.

Bed-wetting (medically known as nocturnal enuresis) is another physical condition related to sleep. Though it usually ends in childhood, bed-wetting is a fairly common condition among teenagers. It can be treated effectively in most cases, but it is not something you can treat yourself, so if you have this problem, make an appointment with your doctor.

The first things your doctor will check for are physical problems or infections. Most infections in the urinary tract can be diagnosed easily with a urine sample. If bed-wetting is not the result of a physical problem or an infection, it is usually caused by one of two other things. One is a bladder so small that it can't hold the quantity of urine produced during the night. The other is very deep sleep. You may sleep so deeply that you don't respond to the physical cues of a full bladder by waking up and going to the bathroom.

Teenage bed wetters with small bladders usually have to urinate frequently during the day. Those who are very deep sleepers don't have any symptoms during the day.

Each of these problems is treated differently. Conditioned-response therapy is generally used for teenagers who have a normal bladder capacity. An alarm buzzer triggered by a small amount of urine wakes the sleeper, who then goes to the bathroom. After a while, he or she learns to respond to a full bladder and wakes up before wetting the bed. Bed wetters who have small bladders are usually given both exercises to enlarge bladder capacity and medication to improve the ability of the bladder to hold urine during the night.

Because help is available, there's no need for anyone to just put up with a bed-wetting problem and hope to outgrow it eventually.

What if you have no physical problems but just can't seem to sleep? If you can't sleep for a night or two every once in a while, don't worry about it. It won't do you any harm to lose that amount of sleep. If you chronically have trouble getting to sleep or you wake frequently during the night, then there are certain things to try.

1. First, have a physical checkup to make sure you don't have any hidden medical conditions that are causing the problem.

2. Watch what you eat and drink. Cola drinks (diet and regular), coffee, tea, and chocolate all contain caffeine, a stimulant. Stay away from them in the late afternoon and evening if you have trouble sleeping. Some people are especially sensitive to specific foods. If there is any food that seems to be related to your sleeping problem, eliminate it from your diet—no matter how farfetched it seems.

3. Avoid beer, wine, or hard liquor at night. Although a small amount of alcohol seems to help in bringing on sleep, it will actually make sleep fitful and shorten REM sleep.

4. L-tryptophan, an amino acid that helps to bring on sleep, is present in high-protein foods such as milk, cheese, turkey, and beef. Try a light snack of one of these foods

before bed. (But keep in mind that a heavy meal before bedtime can sometimes disturb sleep.)

5. If you don't exercise daily, set up a routine of getting some moderate exercise in the late afternoon or early evening (but not just before bed). Try walking, jogging, swimming, skating—anything you like, as long as it's a daily activity.

6. Try a warm bath or shower just before getting into bed. Warmth relaxes muscles and makes you feel drowsy. Make sure your bedroom isn't too warm or too cold, and that there's enough moisture in the air. A temperature between 55 and 65 degrees Fahrenheit, plus relatively high humidity, is best for sleeping. If the air in your room feels dry and static electricity is a problem, use a vaporizer for a few hours each day to add moisture.

7. Stay away from sleeping pills unless your doctor prescribes them. Sleeping pills interfere with REM sleep and leave you physically exhausted instead of rested. All sleeping pills eventually lose their effectiveness, so if you use them, you'll have to take more and more, and they'll have less and less effect.

If none of these things helps, ask your doctor for further suggestions or for a referral to a sleep-disorder clinic. These clinics are located at medical centers around the country, and the doctors who work in them specialize in tracking down the causes of sleep problems.

POSTURE AND PROBLEMS OF
BONES AND MUSCLES

What holds you up? Imagine balancing twenty-four small blocks one on top of the other. Then attach them to each other with some rubber bands and expect that whole structure to bend, sway, support a head, and come through dancing lessons, football scrimmages, and roller-skating sessions in as good condition as it started. Now you can begin to appreciate your spine.

Humans stand upright and walk on two legs—a posture that has many advantages. But it also causes problems such as aches and pains, backache, leg pains, strains and sprains —and, when you're a teenager, constant reminders about "proper" posture.

Your posture is influenced by many things—some physical, such as injuries and heredity, and some emotional. If you feel sad, as if you have the weight of the world on your shoulders, you'll probably stand that way. If you feel happy, your body will show it and you'll walk that way. If you've suddenly grown taller than your friends, you may feel self-conscious about it and try to shrink so you'll be less conspicuous. The result is that you slump. On the other hand, if your friends have suddenly all grown taller than you, you may stand straighter than you ever did to try to look taller.

Just what is good posture? Certainly not the stance of a soldier at attention. That old advice to stand up straight, pull back your shoulders, and tuck in your chin is bad advice. Standing this way is about the worst thing you can do—it only puts a strain on your spine.

The key to good posture is your head. If you push the top of your head toward the ceiling and pull back your chin *slightly,* you'll feel a tendency to pull in your stomach muscles. Then tilt your pelvis forward just a bit, shrug your shoulders up to your ears and drop them behind your earlobes—and you'll be standing the way you should.

Slouching occasionally at this time of your life won't hurt you physically, but it makes you look sloppier and less attractive than if you stand correctly. Poor posture won't cause you any pain now, either, because your body is flexible, but it can lead to problems later on in life, when your spine is less pliable.

If the spine were straight, with each of its twenty-four vertebrae neatly placed one above the next, none of us would ever have any trouble. But if you were to look at it from the side, you'd see that your spine forms three curves. The curve in the middle of your back supports the rib cage and is there when you're born. The other two curves, the neck curve and the lower-back curve, develop when you learn to hold up your head and to walk. Most back pain can be traced to the lower-back curve, known as the lumbar lordosis. When it's exaggerated, this curve is commonly called "swayback."

Each vertebra is separated from the one above it and the one below by fluid-filled disks that absorb shocks. Because their spines are very supple, most teenagers don't have persistent backaches. Anyone can bend the wrong way or slip, however. If this happens and you are having pain or spasms, try using an ice pack for ten to twenty minutes at a time every two hours for the first two days after the injury. Some doctors say this treatment should bring down the swelling and soothe the area—but other doctors feel that rest is the only thing that will help.

If you feel aches and pains in your lower back that aren't due to a sudden injury, you may be able to relieve them by easing the lower-back curve a bit. You can do this by squatting and putting your arms around your knees, or by lying on your side and drawing your knees to your chest. Do this several times a day, for a few minutes each time.

No matter how good your posture, you'll feel miserable if your feet hurt. Never buy shoes that don't fit comfortably when you try them on. No matter what the salesperson says and no matter how good they look, they're unlikely to "stretch out," "ease up," or "loosen" without causing your feet a good deal of pain. It's not worth it.

Your feet will be better off if you change your shoes for another pair at least once during the day, and if you go barefoot for a while each day whenever possible to exercise different groups of muscles in your feet and legs.

If your shoes are comfortable and if you don't wear the same type of shoe all day every day, a specific style won't hurt your feet or deform the foot bones. Sneakers aren't any worse for your feet than lace-up shoes or boots. The two points to remember are that shoes should be comfortable, and should be changed for another style at least once a day.

Blisters are one result of shoes that don't fit well. The top layer of skin becomes separated from the lower layer, and fluid fills the area. Blisters shouldn't be broken by peeling away the top layer of skin. This leaves the lower layer unprotected and slows healing. If you have a blister, you can pierce the top of it with a sterilized needle and gently squeeze out the fluid. (To sterilize a needle, hold it in the flame of a match for two or three seconds.) Dab the blister with antiseptic and put a Band-Aid over it until it heals.

It's always a good idea to break in your shoes gradually.

Wear them around the house for an hour the first day you have them, and increase the time an hour each day for three or four days. Make sure, too, that your socks fit well and don't bunch up in your shoes. No matter how well your shoes fit, socks that are wrinkled up in them will rub the skin of your feet and will probably cause blisters.

Both muscles and bones are growing rapidly during the teen years, and there is a good deal of wear and tear on them; this results in some problems typical of this period of life.

Pain in the front of the knee is common, and occurs when bones are growing rapidly. One leg or both may be affected. Usually you feel a sharp pain just below the kneecap, but you don't remember injuring your leg. The area just below the kneecap will hurt considerably if you tap it, or if you run or jump. These symptoms are typical of a common condition called Osgood-Schlatter disease, which doctors now think is the result of small fractures of the area, where the bone grows longer during childhood and adolescence. The condition is temporary and usually heals by itself.

If you have Osgood-Schlatter disease, your doctor will probably recommend that you stay away from vigorous sports for a period of a few weeks to several months, so the area will have a chance to heal. If you do this, recurrence is rare and you can resume all your usual sports activities. Even if you have to stop other sports for a while, doctors will usually allow swimming if it doesn't bother you. You have a built-in signal to tell you if you're doing too much: pain. If it hurts when you put pressure on the area below your kneecap, you're doing too much and will have to limit your activity more.

Pain in your hip, thigh, or groin or in the area above the knee may signal that the epiphysis (the lengthening tip of the bone) that fits into the hip socket has slipped out of its normal position. This condition is called "a slipped capital femoral epiphysis." Overweight boys are the most likely, but not the only, candidates for this condition.

Usually the pain, which is mild at first, is blamed on a sports injury or accident. It doesn't go away, however, but becomes progressively more bothersome. After a few days the pain may be such that you start to limp. If the condition isn't treated, the limp may become permanent. If you have any hip or thigh pain, or a limp that isn't explained by an injury or strain and that lasts for more than a few days, make an appointment with your doctor.

Scoliosis is another skeletal problem that may appear in teenagers. Scoliosis is a side-to-side curvature of the spine; it's most common in teenage girls. Scoliosis seems to be a hereditary condition, but many teenagers who have it can find no family history of the problem. Some of the first signs of this condition are uneven shoulders or hips, or hemlines that hang crookedly. In a small number of cases, scoliosis gets progressively worse as you grow; in most, it does not. Because scoliosis doesn't cause any discomfort or pain, and because it's difficult to see your own back, it's easy to miss the first symptoms.

Once it's diagnosed, scoliosis should be treated to prevent the curve from becoming more pronounced and causing serious deformities. Treatment can range from special exercises to a special brace, depending on how serious the curve is and what stage of growth you are in. In rare cases, surgery may be necessary.

A different and less serious kind of scoliosis is associated with poorly developed muscles or with legs that differ in length. This kind of curvature does not get progressively worse, and it usually doesn't cause problems. Exercises and shoe height corrected for the difference in leg length are usually all that are necessary. (Incidentally, not everyone has legs that are equal in length. It's common for one leg to be shorter than the other, and differences of up to half an inch usually don't cause any problems.)

During the teen years, strains and sprains are common consequences of participating in sports activities. A strain is an injury to a muscle. A sprain is an injury to a ligament, the connection between two bones.

The best thing for both strains and sprains is to put an ice pack on the injured area as soon as possible. If you don't have an ice pack, put some crushed ice in a damp towel and fold the towel to make a pack the size of the injured area. The ice pack may cause discomfort for the first two or three minutes, but within five minutes the area will become numb. Keep the ice pack on for about ten to twenty minutes and then take it off for an hour. Repeat this several times for the first two days after the injury. The cold will help stop internal bleeding and will also help reduce swelling in the injured area.

After the first two days, switch to wet-heat treatments. (If you use heat before this, you increase the chance of swelling.) Use a wet-heat pack, a moist-heat heating pad, or towels wrung out in hot water. Be careful that none of these is hot enough to burn you. You want the injured area to feel comfortably warm, not burning hot. Apply the heat for about twenty minutes every hour.

Shin splints are a special form of muscle strain that are usually felt as throbbing pain in the lower part of the legs. They're characterized by tenderness and pain of the lower leg muscles, especially along the shin. Sometimes the calf of the leg is tender and the calf muscles are tight. Shin splints hurt when you're active and one leg or both legs may be affected. The best thing to do for shin splints is to apply moist heat. If you're a runner, you may be able to avoid a recurrence of shin splints by wearing shoes or sneakers with cushioned heels and soles, and running or jogging only on a soft track or grass, not on a hard surface like a sidewalk. Shin splints occur in sports other than running. If you suffer from shin splints that don't feel better in a few weeks, see your doctor.

INFECTIOUS DISEASES

Illnesses are frightening. Suddenly, the body you count on to do what you want it to doesn't respond in the way you expect. It changes, sometimes in disturbing ways, and keeps you from doing all you'd like to do and being as active as you want to be—at least temporarily.

Obviously, there are differences between a head cold that keeps you in bed for two days and mononucleosis, which can keep you in bed for two weeks or longer. But both illnesses mean that, for a while at least, you're going to have to pay more attention to how you treat your body. You may have to take medicine, you may have to rest more, and you may have to stay home from school.

Teenagers can develop practically any disease known to

93

medical science, because age is no protection against infection. There are some diseases, however, that affect teenagers more than other age groups, and some diseases that are as common among teenagers as among adults.

As a child, you probably received injections to protect you against several diseases that may be very dangerous and are a nuisance at best. These injections, called immunizations, stimulate the body's immune system to build its own protection against certain diseases. Most children in this country receive a series of three immunizations before they reach their first birthday. Called DPT inoculation, these injections protect against diphtheria, pertussis (whooping cough), and tetanus (lockjaw). A booster shot is given about a year later and then again four years later. If, as a teenager, you're exposed to someone with diphtheria or you plan to travel to parts of the world where diphtheria is not under control, you'll need a booster injection. Otherwise, the immunizations for diphtheria that you received as a child will protect you sufficiently. Whooping cough immunization doesn't need to be repeated after childhood. Tetanus booster injections are given every ten years, unless you get a wound that might be infected with tetanus germs. In that case, if it's been more than five years since you had a booster, you should have another one. Tetanus germs are commonly found in city streets and anyplace where horse or cow manure is present. The rust on a rusty piece of metal is not a problem in itself, but if the piece of metal has been lying in a street or around a farm, chances are good that it's contaminated with tetanus germs.

You were probably also immunized against polio when you were a child. If there's no record of whether you've received the three required doses of polio vaccine, and neither you nor your parents remember whether you did, it would be a good idea to take the entire series of three again. Even if you've had polio vaccine before, you'll do no harm to your body by taking it again. Polio vaccine is given either orally (Sabin) or by injection (Salk). Either series is acceptable.

You may also have received immunizations against measles, mumps, and rubella (German measles). But the measles vaccine that protected you as a child may not still protect you now. Talk to your doctor about whether to get a booster injection. Mumps immunization probably lasts for life. If you've never been vaccinated against mumps and haven't had the disease, you should receive the single injection necessary to protect you, especially if you're a boy. Males can become sterile if they get mumps as adults.

Teenage boys probably don't need to be immunized against rubella even if they haven't had the disease, but girls definitely should be. Most girls are immunized routinely. If for some reason you've never received a rubella immunization and you've never had the disease, you should see a doctor about getting the immunization now. If you get rubella early in pregnancy, your baby is likely to have serious birth defects. Therefore, all girls should be protected long before they plan to have children. Some states, in fact, require proof of immunity to rubella as a condition for getting a marriage license. A simple blood test will tell whether you're immune or not.

Though immunizations can protect you against diseases like rubella and mumps, there are no immunizations for the most common infectious diseases among teenagers: infectious mononucleosis, hepatitis, and mycoplasma pneumonia.

Infectious mononucleosis, usually called "mono," affects teenagers and young adults more than any other age group. Mono is caused by a virus called the Epstein-Barr (EB) virus. In the past, mono was called "the kissing disease" because doctors thought you could get it only by very close contact with someone who had it. Today we know that that's not true, but scientists are still debating how the disease actually is spread.

The first symptoms of mono are usually a slight fever, fatigue, a sore throat, and lack of energy. Other symptoms may include swollen glands, puffy eyelids, and a rash. Quite often, you won't suspect mono, because the symptoms could be caused by any "bug" that's going around or even by lack of sleep. But if you don't feel better even after a few nights of getting to bed early and a few days of taking it easy, then it's time to see a doctor. A simple blood test can make the diagnosis definite.

A lot of misinformation about mono gets spread around. Many teenagers think it's a disabling disease that is difficult to treat. Actually, the acute symptoms, such as fever and sore throat, disappear within a week to ten days, and the lack of energy and fatigue usually disappear within two weeks to a month.

The only treatment for mono is rest and a good diet. Because it's caused by a virus, antibiotics won't help—they act only against bacteria. Usually, you'll find it easy to rest as much as you need to when you have mono, because you'll tire so easily. Though being active won't make mono worse, you just won't feel like doing much for a while.

Mono may enlarge the spleen, an organ located in the upper part of the abdomen that functions as a blood filter. If your spleen enlarges, your doctor will probably limit contact sports such as hockey, football, and soccer until it returns to normal size. (If you're hit in the chest or abdomen while your spleen is enlarged, you risk rupturing it. A rupture would make emergency surgery necessary.)

Complications of mono are extremely rare, and, once you've had the disease, you won't get it again.

The most common type of pneumonia to affect teenagers, mycoplasma pneumonia, causes symptoms that, in the beginning, are very much like the symptoms of mono: headache, sore throat, fever, fatigue, and, after a few days, a cough. The symptoms generally become more severe each day. Teenagers who have mycoplasma pneumonia usually see a doctor after a week or so because they feel so terrible. If nothing is done for the disease, it usually will clear up by itself in another week and you'll start feeling better. The fatigue and the cough can last for several more weeks, but they gradually go away. Antibiotics can shorten the period during which you feel ill and thus allow you to get back to normal activities sooner, but you may tire easily for a while even after other symptoms disappear.

Two types of infectious hepatitis affect teenagers; both are caused by viruses. Type A hepatitis is usually transmitted by eating contaminated food, while type B hepatitis is usually acquired from contaminated blood products or syringes, or from very intimate contact with a person who has the disease. Hepatitis is an inflammation of the liver, which becomes enlarged and tender as the disease progresses.

Both types of hepatitis start with the same symptoms: fatigue, loss of appetite, nausea, and vomiting. As the hepatitis becomes worse, joint pains and chills and fever may occur. Many teenagers who smoke find that cigarettes start to taste strange to them. As the hepatitis progresses further, the urine becomes dark and the skin may take on a yellowish tinge. This yellowing of the skin is called jaundice, and it is at its worst between the first and second week; then it starts fading. It's common for people with hepatitis to become depressed and discontented.

Rest and a good diet are the only treatment for hepatitis. Drinking enough liquids is important, as it is with any other illness. Convalescence usually lasts for several weeks, during which time appetite and a rosier view of the world gradually return.

There is another group of infectious diseases for which there are no immunizations; these are diseases spread by sexual contact. Traditionally, these have been called venereal disease, or VD, but today, doctors often prefer to call them sexually transmissible diseases or sexually transmitted diseases—STDs.

VD is sometimes thought of as one disease, but, actually, several diseases—including gonorrhea, syphilis, nonspecific urethritis, genital herpes, venereal warts, and vaginitis—are all "VD."

First, some facts about VD in general. Some of the diseases that make up the category can be transmitted only through close sexual contact, because the organisms responsible for them will survive only in the warm, moist atmosphere the sex organs provide. Others can also be transmitted by other kinds of close physical contact. None of them can be "caught," like a cold or the measles, from being in the same room with someone who has VD.

Venereal disease is serious! In the early stages there may be no symptoms, but if VD is left untreated, serious and often irreversible damage to the body can occur. VD is nothing to stick your head in the sand about, and you can't just hope it will go away, because it won't. It may go into hiding, that's all.

Gonorrhea (also called "the clap") is probably the most widespread venereal disease. Statistically, it occurs most often among young adults (those twenty to twenty-four years old), but the next largest number of cases occurs among adolescents fifteen to nineteen years old. People of any age can catch the disease, however, so if you're under fifteen, don't think you're immune. And, if you've had gonorrhea once, you may still get it again, because your body builds up no immunity to it. Some people get gonorrhea over and over again from the same untreated sex partner.

Gonorrhea is transmitted only by sexual contact, because the bacteria that cause it cannot survive anywhere but in the human body. You cannot get gonorrhea from towels, drinking glasses, or toilet seats, though some people may try to convince you otherwise.

The symptoms of gonorrhea can appear as soon as one day or as late as a month after sexual contact with an infected person. Boys usually develop symptoms within three to six days. The earliest symptoms are a discharge from the penis and burning on urination. The discharge may be heavy or light, but usually it is pus-laden. Unfortunately, girls often have no symptoms at all. Sometimes girls have burning when they urinate, a vaginal discharge, or pain in the lower abdomen, but this happens in only a minority of cases, and often is ignored. Because girls can be infected and not develop any symptoms, it's important that a boy who is diagnosed as having gonorrhea *tell his sex partner* so that she can get treatment. Untreated gonorrhea in both males and females can eventually result in sterility, and may also spread through the body to affect the joints with a kind of arthritis.

Gonorrhea of the throat can occur after oral/genital contact, and gonorrhea of the rectum may follow anal intercourse. Often there are no symptoms in these two instances, and the only way to be sure whether you have gonorrhea is to be tested for it.

The test for gonorrhea is simple. A sample of the discharge is examined under a microscope to see if gonococci—the bacteria that cause the disease—are present. If there is no discharge, a culture is taken from any possible site of infection. This doesn't hurt; a cotton-tipped swab is just touched to the area. The material on the swab is transferred to a dish and is cultured for a short time; then it is examined for the presence of gonococci.

Penicillin is the usual treatment for gonorrhea, but if you're sensitive to penicillin (or if you happen to have a penicillin-resistant type of gonorrhea), other antibiotics can be used.

Syphilis is not as common as gonorrhea these days, but it's still a problem. Syphilis is caused by spiral-shaped bacteria that are transmitted through sexual contact. In rare instances, these bacteria may enter an open cut in the skin during contact with an infected sex organ; they may also be transmitted by kissing if there is a syphilis sore on the lips or mouth.

Syphilis appears in stages. The first stage, which develops after an average incubation period of three weeks, is a sore called a chancre that's usually inconspicuous and painless. A chancre may look like a pimple, but it often feels hard and looks as if it's been punched out in the center. The chancre usually disappears in a few weeks. This does *not* mean that the disease is cured; it simply means it's gone into hiding. And though you don't have any symptoms, you can still give syphilis to your sex partners at this stage.

The next stage generally appears within six months, and the symptoms are noticeable: headache, sore throat, slight fever, swollen glands, and, finally, a painless red rash covering the entire body, including the palms of the hands and the soles of the feet. Syphilis is usually diagnosed at this stage, because the rash is hard to ignore. If the disease is left untreated, however, the rash will clear up and the syphilis will go into hiding again until the third stage appears, sometimes years later. Tragically, at this stage the disease causes brain and heart damage.

Syphilis can be diagnosed from a sample scraped from a chancre, or with a blood test called the VDRL test (after the Venereal Disease Research Laboratory), four to six weeks after contact with someone who has the disease. It can be completely cured by penicillin, or by other drugs if you're allergic to penicillin. Early treatment is important, so if you find any sores around your genital area or rectum that could be the result of sexual contact, have them checked.

Nonspecific urethritis (NSU), also called nongonococcal urethritis (NGU), is usually caused by organisms called chlamydia that have properties of both viruses and bacteria, although it can also be caused by other organisms. The disease usually produces symptoms in boys, but both boys and girls can have it and not develop symptoms. NSU can be confused with gonorrhea because the symptoms are the same: in boys, a discharge from the penis and pain when urinating; in girls, a slight vaginal discharge or pain when urinating. Symptoms usually appear (if they appear at all) a week or two after infection. Diagnosis is done by testing for both gonorrhea and syphilis. If both tests are negative, then those two diseases are ruled out and NSU is assumed.

NSU is usually treated with the antibiotic tetracycline. There are few complications of the disease, but if your sex partner is infected and not treated, you're likely to be reinfected.

Herpes simplex, type 1, is a virus that causes cold sores and fever blisters. A similar type of herpes virus, type 2, causes genital herpes, painful blisters on and around the sex organs. Doctors used to think that type 1 appeared above the waist and type 2 below the waist, but we now know that both strains can appear on any part of the body.

The herpes virus is passed by direct contact with the blisters or the sores that result after the blisters break. (If you do have genital herpes, it's important not to spread it, so avoid sexual contact any time that blisters or sores are present.)

Genital herpes may appear three to twenty days after sexual contact with an infected person, but not always. The virus can go dormant after the incubation period, and blisters may not appear until several years after the initial contact. When the blisters do appear, they are very painful, but they break and then heal within three weeks without any treatment. Unfortunately, this doesn't mean the end of the disease. Genital herpes can keep coming back. Usually there's a second very painful attack within six months of the original one. After that, each successive attack becomes milder, and the attacks also become less frequent. The pattern and location of the blisters are the same every time the infection recurs. Recurrences seem to be triggered by stress or illness.

At this time, there is no cure for genital herpes (though there are several treatments that look promising). But there are things you can do to make a herpes attack less uncomfortable. Keep the infected area dry and as clean as possible, to promote healing. Wear loose cotton underwear, and avoid tight clothing and clothing made of synthetic fabrics, which will trap moisture. If the blisters are extremely painful, your doctor can prescribe an ointment that will help to control the pain.

Venereal warts (condylomata acuminata) appear on the genitals and are also caused by a virus. During sexual intercourse, the virus passes from the genital area of one partner to that of the other. Venereal warts look frightening, like miniature cauliflowers, but they are not hard to get rid of, and rarely cause any serious complications. Don't wait for venereal warts to disappear by themselves, and don't try to deal with them yourself—see your doctor. Doctors usually use one of three treatments: a medication that will destroy the warts, an electric needle to remove them, or liquid nitrogen to freeze them. All three methods are effective, and the one your doctor chooses will depend on your individual case.

Vaginitis, inflammation of the vagina, is a general name given to three different conditions caused by three different organisms. Moniliasis is caused by a yeastlike fungus; trichomoniasis is caused by a parasite; and nonspecific vaginitis is caused by bacteria. All three are accompanied by a very obvious symptom—itching—and all are associated with an abnormal vaginal discharge. Normally, most vaginal discharges vary from clear to whitish. If there's an infection, the discharge will be a peculiar color, or will be frothy or have an unpleasant odor. Vaginitis is usually easily and effectively treated, and complications are rare. If you think you have vaginitis, see your doctor.

There *are* ways to prevent the spread of VD. One of the most important is not to assume it can't happen to you. VD does get around—it's a major health problem of epidemic proportions. If you notice any symptoms, or if you know you've been exposed to any of the sexually transmissible diseases, call your local health department's VD clinic. Minors can be treated without the consent of their parents, and if you go to a health department VD clinic, you can be sure your case will be kept completely confidential. It's actually against the law for any of these clinics to divulge information about you to anyone. The doctors and nurses on the staff see a lot of different diseases and a lot of different kinds of people. They're not interested in giving you lectures about your life-style. They *are* interested in stopping the epidemic spread of VD. Most clinics offer no-cost or low-cost diagnosis and treatment.

If you'd rather go to your family doctor but are afraid he or she might tell your parents about your visit, ask your doctor, "Would you tell my parents about anything I come to you about, without my permission?" You don't have to mention what the problem is to find out if your visits would be considered confidential.

If you are diagnosed as having VD, *it's very important to tell your sex partners,* even if it's a hard thing to do. You may save someone else from a serious illness.

Finally, if you have any questions about VD or about where to get help, call the VD National Hotline. This is a toll-free call—in other words, it won't cost you anything—and you don't have to give your name. The number is 800-227-8922 except in California, where it's 800-892-5883. Someone is there to take your call from eight A.M. to eight P.M. (Pacific Time) Monday through Friday, and from ten A.M. to six P.M. (Pacific Time) on Saturday and Sunday.

DRUGS

We hear a lot of talk these days about "the drug problem."
According to some people, anyone who uses any illegal drug
should be thrown in jail. According to others, all drugs
should be made legal and available on demand. These two
opposite viewpoints, and those that fall in between, involve
moral, ethical, and legal questions that are outside the scope
of a book on health. This chapter can only deal with drugs
from a medical standpoint. It will consider the physical
consequences of drug use and will briefly explain what we
know about how drugs affect the body and mind. As you'll
see, that alone is enough to make a rather long chapter, for
there are so many different kinds of drugs to consider.

When people talk about drug abuse or drug misuse, they

usually have in mind drugs that alter awareness—how you think, how you feel, and how you behave. These drugs are called psychoactive, because they alter the way the brain functions. Many drugs that are used medically aren't psychoactive—they affect parts of the body other than the brain. A drug, by definition, is any substance that produces a physical, psychological, or emotional change in the user. Aspirin is a drug; penicillin is a drug; and so are nicotine, heroin, and alcohol.

There is some risk involved in the use of any drug, including such a common one as penicillin. The benefits from its use far outweigh the risks, however. It's more important to be able to control strep throat in many thousands of people than to ban penicillin because some people are allergic to it.

In general, whether the use of a drug is legal or illegal in today's society depends on whether the benefits of its use outweigh the risks. There are exceptions, of course. Alcohol and nicotine, two of the most harmful drugs, are legal to use in spite of the fact that there are serious risks involved. Alcohol has some use medically, and, when it is used occasionally and moderately in nonmedical ways, it usually doesn't cause any harmful side effects. It does have a great potential for harm, however. Nicotine has always been a legal drug even though it has no practical use in medicine, is of no physical benefit, and may cause grave physical damage to users.

There are many reasons why people use the controversial

psychoactive drugs. The reason most often given for using drugs is "to feel better." This usually means to achieve a "high," a time when cares recede. It means using something *external,* something swallowed, inhaled, sniffed, or injected, to relieve *internal* pressure.

There's nothing wrong with seeking relief from pressure. Many people meditate or listen to music or go to the movies to relax. But finding relief through drugs usually means paying a considerable personal price. Drugs—from cigarettes to alcohol to marijuana to heroin—are crutches to help you get through uncomfortable situations. And sometimes crutches shouldn't be used, even if you feel unsteady without them. Using drugs doesn't solve the problem or change the situation, so the high helps only for a brief time. And drug use can become an end in itself, causing personal development and psychological growth to suffer at a crucial stage of your life. The reason psychoactive drugs are generally illegal is that the risks of using them do outweigh the benefits.

Whether or not to use drugs, or how to use them, is a personal choice. Most people who have used drugs will tell you the benefits they see. Whether to use drugs is a choice you have to make for yourself—but before you make it, you'd better know the risks involved as well as the supposed benefits.

Earlier in this century, saloons put out dishes of cold cuts, pickled eggs, salads, and bread for patrons to eat when they bought a drink. This was called a "free lunch," and the term came to mean getting something for nothing. As far as drugs go, there is no free lunch. There's no drug potent enough to cause pleasure that doesn't also carry with it some element of risk.

Drugs used for their psychoactive properties can be classified by the way in which they affect the user. They include hallucinogens, narcotics, stimulants, sedative/hypnotics, and inhalants. Alcohol (a sedative/hypnotic), tobacco (a stimulant), and marijuana (a hallucinogen) are usually discussed separately because of their widespread use.

In some cases, the more a drug is used, the more of it you need to achieve the original effect; nothing happens unless the dose is increased. In that case, we say that *tolerance* to the drug develops. People often develop a tolerance to the effects of alcohol, for instance, so that after a while a drinker has to have two or three beers to get the same feeling of relaxation he or she used to get with one.

Tolerance usually accompanies *dependence.* People who are dependent need to have the drug not just to get high or to become relaxed, but to function normally. Drug dependence can be physical or psychological, or both. Dependence usually results from continued use of a drug.

If you are physically dependent on a drug, withdrawal symptoms occur when the drug is discontinued. As your body adjusts to use of the drug, changes occur in the cells that make up the central nervous system. When you stop using the drug, your body has to readjust to its absence, and symptoms such as sweating, shaking, insomnia, and rapid heartbeat occur while your body is readjusting.

Any drug that can alter mood favorably or create a pleasant state of mind can induce psychological dependence—a compulsion to use the drug repeatedly even though there are no physical changes in the central nervous system. If you're psychologically dependent, it means you are convinced that you won't be able to function or feel good without the drug. Sometimes the physical and psychological aspects of dependence are so intertwined that it's difficult to tell which is which.

Hallucinogens

Hallucinogens (also called psychedelics) are drugs that alter the way you perceive reality. They change your usual sense of time and space and seem to sharpen your senses of smell, hearing, touch, taste, and sight. People taking hallucinogens say they can "hear" color and "see" music. All hallucinogens produce their effect by interfering with the way the brain normally works. Though perception is always altered consciousness may or may not remain clear.

Everyone responds differently to hallucinogens. The same dose of the same drug will cause some people to become quietly happy, while it will make others feel panicky and disturbed. No one can tell you how you'll react, because your reaction will depend on several things, including the purity of the drug, how much you take, your physical surroundings, and your own physical and psychological condition. People often do not respond to the same hallucinogen in the same way each time they take it.

Hallucinogens are usually divided into two groups: those that come from plants, and those that are chemically produced.

Hallucinogens that come from plants include certain varieties of morning glory seeds, mescaline (from peyote cactus buttons), psilocybin (from a mushroom that grows in Mexico), and nutmeg.

LSD (lysergic acid diethylamide), also known as "acid," is the most common laboratory-made hallucinogen. A dose the size of a speck of dust can send the user on a "trip" lasting anywhere from eight to twelve hours. LSD acts directly on the brain without causing loss of consciousness. As with other hallucinogens, the experience may vary widely from one person to the next, and from one trip to another for any one person. Some people can take LSD and have nothing but wonderful experiences, while others have bad trips as often as good ones.

One of the worst dangers with LSD is that it may not be pure. A dealer may try to increase his stock by diluting it, and the chances for a bad trip are greatly increased if the LSD is mixed with something else.

Never use LSD when you're alone. If you use it, make sure the person with you has had some experience with it. One reason to have someone with you is that LSD can make you feel as though you can't be harmed—people have jumped out of windows or run in front of cars while they were on LSD trips. Another reason not to be alone is that if you do have a bad trip, it's best to have someone "talk you down"—that is, constantly reassure you until the effects of the LSD wear off. This is best done by someone you trust completely who knows what's happening to you.

LSD users can experience flashbacks. A flashback is a frightening, unexpected repetition of a trip (either bad or good) that takes place months or even years after the original trip. Flashbacks may result from taking some medicine, such as an antihistamine; from smoking marijuana; or from stress. Or they may occur spontaneously, out of the clear blue sky.

PCP (phencyclidine) is another laboratory-made hallucinogen; it's also known as "angel dust." Its effects are similar to those of LSD, but PCP also has some hypnotic effects. PCP was originally developed as an anesthetic, but because of unpleasant side effects, it was withdrawn from medical use with humans.

PCP is a dangerous drug because its effects are completely unpredictable and because it can produce violent behavior even in people who are normally calm. The violence may be directed at others, but the user may also turn on himself or herself, and this sometimes leads to suicide. Even moderate doses of PCP can cause people to temporarily lose contact with reality and to show all the signs of severe mental illness.

It is the only hallucinogen that may cause a coma, and an overdose may cause death.

Tolerance to hallucinogens can develop very quickly— sometimes after as little as three days of regular use—and more and more will be needed to produce the desired results. Hallucinogens don't cause physical dependence and there are no withdrawal symptoms, but psychological dependence does occur.

Marijuana and Hashish

Marijuana (pot, grass, weed, MJ) and hashish (hash) both come from the cannabis plant. The active ingredient in them is delta-9-tetrahydrocannabinol, or THC. There's been a great deal of controversy about the effects of marijuana and hashish on health, and for good reason: knowledge about long-term effects is scanty because the drug hasn't been widely enough used for a long enough time for doctors to study it carefully. (After all, it was only after fifty years of widespread use that we discovered some of the long-term effects of cigarettes.) One thing we do know is that marijuana and hashish are *not* completely harmless substances. Solid medical research shows some reasons to be very wary about using them.

Cannabis preparations can be smoked as marijuana "joints" or eaten in the form of "hash oil" added to foods, usually baked goods. The amount of THC your body absorbs will depend on how you take the drug. In the United States, smoking marijuana is the commonest way of using cannabis. It's also the most potent—smoking delivers THC to the brain within fourteen seconds of inhaling.

THC is fat-soluble—that is, fat cells and organs in the body soak it up after it enters the bloodstream. It accumulates in body fat, and, as a result, a regular user faces an increased risk from the effects of THC because the body is never fully rid of it. THC remains in the body for up to thirty days; therefore, even if you smoke only one joint a week, you have a constant, active level of THC in your body.

Marijuana is a hallucinogen. When smoked, the effects of one joint can last for two or three hours. It usually produces feelings of relaxation and euphoria, and for most users it alters perceptions of distance and time. Some users react badly, however, with feelings of panic and even hallucinations. This kind of reaction is most likely to occur if you're anxious or under stress, or if you take stronger marijuana than usual without knowing it. These symptoms usually disappear when the drug wears off.

Sometimes marijuana users experience mild paranoid feelings—that is, they think that everyone's against them. This kind of reaction is more likely to occur if you're anxious about smoking itself or about where you're smoking (for example, if you're smoking at home, where a disapproving parent is likely to walk in).

A lot of the negative psychological effects of marijuana are caused by marijuana that is "too strong"—that is, stronger than you are used to. Street marijuana has become stronger in the last five years, and, because the potency varies according to the source, there's no way of telling beforehand whether you'll be getting the strength you're used to. (Another problem related to source is that, increasingly, marijuana is coming through contaminated with PCP.)

Marijuana can affect intellectual performance and learning. There's no longer any question that smoking marijuana impairs short-term memory, so if you try to learn something when you're high, you won't recall it as well as you would if you studied it in an undrugged state. And if you smoke after you finish studying, it will affect your memory for that material.

Because it affects reaction time, judgment, and concentration, marijuana also affects driving ability. It's generally unsafe to drive for at least three hours after smoking. A routine saliva test similar to the Breathalyzer test for drunk drivers is now being developed to detect marijuana-intoxicated drivers. Once this test becomes routine, the penalties for driving while intoxicated by marijuana will probably be at least as severe as those for driving while intoxicated by alcohol.

Smoking marijuana has physical as well as psychological effects. Though scientists are still debating the long-term significance of some of the physical changes that take place, there is one area about which there is no debate. It has been proven that daily use of marijuana leads to lung damage. Smoking less than one joint a day affects your vital capacity (the amount of air you can exhale from your lungs after a deep breath) as much as smoking sixteen cigarettes a day. One joint also yields twice as much tar as an ordinary cigarette. The tar in both marijuana and cigarette tobacco is cancer-producing, and smoking two or three joints a day carries with it the same risk of lung damage as smoking a pack of cigarettes a day, because joints are smoked to the very end. Marijuana smokers often develop the same hoarseness, cough, and inflammation of the bronchial tubes that cigarette smokers develop—but at a much earlier age.

It's not too surprising that smoking marijuana has a physical effect on the lungs and breathing capacity. But marijuana also affects other body systems. Scientists generally agree that it is associated with changes in the reproductive organs in both males and females.

Men who use marijuana heavily (smoking eight to twenty joints a day) have lower levels of testosterone, a male sex hormone, than average. At these lower testosterone levels, female sex characteristics such as breast development may occur. There is also a lower sperm count, and there are more abnormally shaped sperm than is normal. This does not mean that sperm production is completely suppressed, however, so heavy marijuana usage should never be considered a substitute for a reliable contraceptive.

Women who use marijuana three times a week or more for at least six months have more irregular menstrual cycles than nonusers. These women may fail to ovulate, and they produce three times as many defective eggs when ovulation does occur. Research in this area is still limited, and we are not yet certain of the possible long-term effects of marijuana on children born to users.

Tolerance to marijuana develops rapidly and is clearly associated with repeated use. The more it's smoked and the higher the dose, the more quickly tolerance develops, but people smoking even one joint a day may develop a tolerance to some of the effects of THC. Mild physical dependence seems to be associated with very heavy marijuana use, and withdrawal symptoms such as irritability, sweating, nausea, and sleep disturbance can show up if the drug is discontinued.

Keep in mind that most of the present medical knowledge about marijuana comes from research with *healthy, adult men.* Some of the changes marijuana brings about may not matter to a healthy adult—but they could matter a great deal to a teenager who is still developing rapidly both physically and psychologically. Because widespread marijuana use is so recent in our society, research results are just starting to come in. Some of the long-term effects won't be known for another thirty to forty years. Until we know more about the effects of marijuana than we do now, we should remain cautious about its use.

Narcotics

Narcotics are drugs that relieve pain and induce a state of euphoria, a sense of general well-being. They cloud consciousness and dull normal physical appetites, such as hunger and sexual desire; they also dull normal feelings such as anger. Narcotics include morphine and heroin, drugs derived from opium; meperidine (Demerol) and methadone, synthetic compounds with morphinelike action; and codeine (also derived from opium). About 90 percent of narcotics abuse in this country is accounted for by heroin.

Narcotics can be sniffed, injected under the skin or into a muscle, or injected directly into a vein ("mainlined"). Many users say that the way the narcotic is used influences the degree of addiction, but scientists aren't sure this is true. ˜

The physical threats to health from narcotics dependence include the dangers of overdose, infection, and contamination. Because there is no control of illegal drugs, narcotics are often mixed with other substances, such as baking soda or quinine, to expand the volume and thereby increase their street value. Those who are dependent on a narcotic can't accurately estimate the necessary dose, if only because the strength of the drug will vary from one batch to the next, so death from overdose is not uncommon. Infections abound among users; they are usually caused by unsterile needles, syringes, and solutions.

All narcotics cause physical dependence. Tolerance to any of them develops with regular use, and lack of the drug causes withdrawal symptoms. Methadone, a synthetic narcotic used in the treatment of some heroin addicts, is not as addicting as heroin because it doesn't produce as much pleasure. However, because methadone is a narcotic, it is physically addicting.

Stimulants

Stimulants act directly on the central nervous system to promote a feeling of alertness. Coffee, tea, and chocolate are all mild stimulants. Drugs used as stimulants are members of the amphetamine family, usually dextroamphetamine (Dexedrine, or "pep pills") or methamphetamine (Methedrine, or "speed"). Someone taking amphetamines feels less tired and more alert; heart rate and blood pressure increase, and appetite declines.

In the past, amphetamines were used medically to control appetite for weight-reduction diets. But the drug works only briefly and the body adjusts to it quickly, so the dose must continually be increased to get the same effect. Amphetamines were always of limited value in controlling appetite, and they are rarely used for that purpose today.

Even infrequent use of amphetamines can produce a bad reaction if you happen to be sensitive to them. Some users report jumpiness, insomnia, irritability, rashes, and headaches. High doses of amphetamines can cause severe fright, hallucinations, and paranoia (the feeling that everyone's against you); sometimes this leads to physical violence or suicide.

Amphetamines are not strongly addicting physically, but users develop an extreme psychological dependence. Withdrawing them after heavy use results in depression and overwhelming fatigue.

Cocaine

Cocaine is considered a stimulant, and its effects are similar to the effects of amphetamines. Cocaine comes from the leaves of the South American coca plant.

People who use cocaine to get high generally "snort" it—inhale it through the nose in the form of a powder. Infrequent, low-dose use presents few physical risks; nasal symptoms are common if cocaine is used moderately or frequently. The most common complaint is a runny nose, but moderate use has been reported to cause inflammation of the nostrils, with sores and bleeding. Prolonged, heavy use may result in erosion of the tissues between the nostrils.

Cocaine constricts the cells in the nasal passage so that only a certain amount can be absorbed when it is inhaled. Because of this, users are now converting it to "free-base" so that it can be inhaled like cigarette smoke. This results in a tremendous high followed quickly by an intense low. The acute depression tends to make people want more cocaine to produce another high. When cocaine is used in this way, the amount that enters the bloodstream is not limited, and the risks increase. Overdose can occur, and may result in coma or even death.

Cocaine is an expensive drug and the readily available supply is always "cut" with something else, so quality is unreliable and the drug may even be dangerous, depending on the substance used to cut it.

Tobacco

If you smoke just one pack of cigarettes, you may be hooked for life—or at least for many years. Until fairly recently, cigarette smoking was considered a bad habit, but one that anyone could control with a little willpower. Recent evidence, however, has shown that cigarette smoking is a stubborn form of drug addiction—the smoker has a true physical dependence on nicotine, which is the active ingredient in tobacco. Nicotine is a powerful drug. You develop a tolerance to it, as well as a physical dependence on it. Addiction is established quickly and easily. If you stop smoking, you will probably have withdrawal symptoms.

Nicotine is a stimulant. Each time cigarette smoke is inhaled, a dose of nicotine is sent from the lungs into the bloodstream. Nicotine acts on specific nerves in the body, stimulating them to release chemicals. These chemicals increase heart rate, raise blood pressure, and narrow blood vessels.

In addition to stimulating the nervous system, the nicotine

in tobacco smoke reaches the brain within ten seconds of inhalation. If the amount of nicotine present in a single cigarette were injected directly into the bloodstream rather than being absorbed through the lungs, it would paralyze the centers in the brain controlling breathing, and would cause death. If each cigarette has about ten puffs in it, a pack-a-day smoker delivers more than 70,000 doses of nicotine to the bloodstream and brain each year.

Cigarette smoke contains carbon monoxide, which interferes with the ability of the red blood cells to carry oxygen. As already noted, nicotine narrows the blood vessels, increases heart rate, and raises blood pressure. The combined effects of nicotine and carbon monoxide guarantee that smokers will not be able to perform as well in athletic competition as nonsmokers. Furthermore, smokers tend to have impaired blood circulation, especially in the hands and feet.

Tolerance to nicotine develops rapidly, as does physical dependence. People also become psychologically dependent on cigarettes. It is astonishing how quickly you can become hooked. For most teenagers, smoking is so addicting that *if you finish smoking one pack of cigarettes by the time you're eighteen, you are almost sure to be a regular smoker for the next forty years.*

Sedative/Hypnotics
Sedative/hypnotics are roughly the opposite of stimulants. They are used to bring on sleep and relieve anxiety. Seda-

tive/hypnotics depress the activity of the central nervous system and of other body systems as well. They slow down heartbeat and breathing, and reduce muscle coordination.

By far the most dangerous of the sedative/hypnotics are barbiturates ("barbs," "reds," "downers"). Nembutal, Seconal, and Fiorinal are all barbiturates. Doctors prescribe them for short-term use in special situations. When they are misused, barbiturates can kill people. Large doses depress the activity of the central nervous system to such a degree that coma and death can result. Lesser doses cause slurred speech, staggering walk, and slowed reaction time. Driving a car or operating machinery after taking barbiturates is very dangerous.

The nonbarbiturate sedative/hypnotics include tranquilizers such as Librium and Valium, and sleeping pills such as Placidyl, Quaalude, Doriden, and Noludar.

If you're taking any sedative/hypnotic drug, *never* drink anything alcoholic while you're using it (this includes beer and wine). The drug and the alcohol will act on each other, multiplying the effect of both substances. The combination can cause coma or even death.

Physical and psychological dependence can result from the misuse of nonbarbiturate sedative/hypnotics, and withdrawal symptoms can be uncomfortable. Barbiturates create physical dependence; some of them are as addictive as narcotics.

Users develop a tolerance for sedative/hypnotic drugs,

needing more and more to achieve the same effect. How quickly tolerance develops, and whether there are withdrawal symptoms, depends on how much of the drug is used. Withdrawal from regular barbiturate use should be done only under a doctor's supervision.

Alcohol

Alcohol is a drug—one of the most abused drugs in this country. Like all the other sedative/hypnotics, alcohol is a central nervous system depressant, and that means that it reduces alertness and impairs motor coordination. Because alcohol acts first on the brain centers that affect self-control, many people who drink believe—incorrectly—that alcohol is a stimulant.

Because alcohol affects self-control, aggressive behavior often results from drinking. Alcohol has the reputation of loosening sexual inhibitions, which it does, and of increasing sexual ability and performance, which it doesn't. Teenagers sometimes drink because they feel insecure about sexual matters. But the sad truth is that because it is a depressant, alcohol can impair sexual functioning.

Alcohol and driving don't mix. You hear that statement so often you may begin to ignore it. But there's a clear reason behind it: alcohol affects reaction time. It also affects perception, so that you may think your senses are sharp and your reaction time is as good as ever when, in fact, both are faulty. Alcohol-related highway accidents are the number-one cause of death among teenagers in this country, and half of *all* highway deaths involve alcohol abuse. Even the driver who escapes death or serious injury in an alcohol-related accident may suffer severe psychological effects.

The suggestion that you make coffee the one for the road makes a nice advertising campaign, but neither cold showers nor coffee can sober you up. Alcohol is eliminated from the bloodstream by the liver, and it takes about an hour for the body to get rid of an ounce of hard liquor. That's the equivalent of about a jigger of whiskey, or eight to twelve ounces of beer, or four ounces of wine.

People develop a tolerance for alcohol, and can become physically dependent on it. But not every drinker becomes dependent on alcohol, and one binge or hangover won't make you an alcoholic. People are said to be dependent if they can't control their drinking, or when drinking results in physical or psychological symptoms. About one out of every ten people who drink will become dependent, but there's no way of telling beforehand who will or will not.

Inhalants

Inhalants are substances that are breathed in to produce the same kind of "buzz" you get from drinking alcohol. Inhalants commonly abused are glue, gasoline, paint thinner, nail-polish remover, and dry-cleaning fluid. Because they have legitimate uses, most people don't think of inhalants as drugs. But using inhalants is risky. If the concentration of oxygen that's breathed in with the inhalant is too low, the user may faint or even suffocate.

Long-term studies have been made of industrial workers exposed to inhalants every working day. These people sustained serious damage to the brain, liver, and blood. What the long-term effects of occasional use are is still not certain, but because using inhalants cuts off the supply of oxygen to the brain, it's likely that some brain damage does occur. Whether inhalants create physical dependence is still not known.

Drug Overdose

An overdose of *any* drug is an amount that produces dangerous reactions—coma, shallow breathing, very slow or very rapid breathing, or stupor. If you or anyone you're with begins to experience these symptoms, don't wait to see if the effects wear off. Get medical help immediately! Go to the nearest emergency room, doctor's office, or medical clinic.

Sometimes hallucinogens or stimulants produce a panic reaction and the user becomes frightened and suspicious of other people. Anyone nearby should speak softly, move slowly, and be quietly reassuring until the effects wear off.

Where To Get Help

If you want help with a drug problem, you can probably find it near your home. Look in your local telephone book for a section headed "Community Services Numbers." Most telephone books have it. Programs for drug problems are listed under "Drugs," or "Alcohol and Drugs," or "Alcohol." If you can't find such a section in your telephone book, call your state or city health department. (You won't have to give your name.) You can be certain that your visit to a clinic or hospital will be kept confidential and won't be reported to your parents or your school. There are now federal regulations that protect your privacy if you seek treatment. Doctors, psychologists, and drug treatment centers must keep any information you give them confidential or face a fine of five thousand dollars.

SEXUAL QUESTIONS

During adolescence, you have to adjust to some of the most extreme physical and emotional changes you will go through during your life. These changes are often confusing, and you may find yourself faced with difficult choices. Some of these choices are intimately bound up with your sexuality in its broadest sense: who you are as a male or female person.

Some people see sexuality as limited to sexual intercourse, or sexual role-playing, or even "sexiness." But sexuality goes far beyond that, and has to do with how you express yourself as a human being throughout your life. How well you accept your sexuality and how comfortable you are with it is a measure of how much you value yourself.

At some point, most teenagers begin to feel needs and

longings for new forms of intimacy and love and acceptance. One way of expressing intimacy is touching. All of us need to be touched, to be held and hugged. Parents hold fretting infants to calm them, toddlers hold out their arms to be picked up if they've been hurt, adults instinctively put their arms around other adults who need to be comforted. Touch —communication without words—is a powerful and necessary part of our lives from infancy to old age.

It's important to recognize the human need to be touched and to touch someone else, and important to recognize that touching is a way of expressing love that is satisfying and valuable in itself. Holding and being held, kissing and being kissed need not lead to sexual intercourse. Sadly enough, too many teenagers find it difficult to realize that love and sexuality can be expressed in many ways, and they may end up engaging in sexual intercourse before they're really ready for it.

There's a lot of pressure on both boys and girls to become sexually active. But no one, boy or girl, should feel pushed into sex. One of the most important choices you'll ever have to make is how to express your own sexuality—from hugging someone to having intercourse. People will probably keep telling you about the "new freedom." But what they often fail to mention is that the new freedom includes the freedom to say no. Anyone who wants to share a relationship with you who isn't willing to take "no" for an answer, or who constantly pressures you to change your mind, isn't trying to share a relationship—he or she is trying to manipulate you. And no one needs that.

The intimacy of a sexual relationship is a whole new dimension of life. Though it's natural to be curious and to want to explore and experiment, there's no need to rush—or to allow yourself to be rushed. Sex can mean different things to different people (and to some people it has very little meaning). You have a right to take your time and decide what it will mean to you. A sexual relationship is the most intimate form of human relationship and the most emotionally demanding. Just because you're physically capable doesn't mean you're emotionally ready. And if you feel you're not ready for this kind of intimacy, you have a right to insist that your involvement be kept on a less intense plane.

You may feel that a relationship is so important that it demands physical expression, and that you're ready for sexual involvement. But however awesome the emotions involved, it would be foolish to forget that sexual intercourse is nature's way of reproducing the human species, and that pregnancy is a natural result of intercourse. And that is not something to be ignored, forgotten, or taken lightly.

Once you have reached puberty, you are as fertile and as capable of fathering a child or conceiving a child as any adult. But that does not necessarily mean that you are emotionally or economically ready to cope with an infant, or to face the changes an infant would make in your life. Nor does it mean that a teenage girl is physically ready for a safe and healthy pregnancy and birth.

A teenage couple who are having sexual intercourse should use a recognized form of contraception if they don't want to deal with pregnancy. Once a girl starts having menstrual periods, she can become pregnant at any time.

Usually a girl releases one egg a month. The exact time of ovulation is difficult to pinpoint even for women who have been menstruating for years and who have absolutely regular menstrual cycles. Ovulation usually occurs in the middle of the menstrual cycle—that is, about two weeks before the next period is due and about two weeks after the last one began (or, if the cycle is longer, ovulation occurs roughly two weeks before the next period). But this varies from woman to woman, and there's no way to state a definite time that applies to every female.

When a man has an orgasm during intercourse, sperm are propelled out of his urethra and into the woman's vagina. From the vagina, the sperm enter the uterus through the cervical opening (the os), and finally they swim into the uterine tubes. If an egg has been released and is in one of the uterine tubes, a sperm can penetrate it and fertilize it. No one knows definitely how long sperm can survive once they are in the uterus, or how long an egg remains fertile once it's been released from an ovary. But some *300 to 500 million sperm* are released in an average ejaculation, and it takes just *one* to fertilize an egg. Furthermore, fertilization can occur several days after intercourse. Because women have been known to become pregnant during any time of the menstrual cycle, no girl can assume she knows her "safe" days.

Some myths about preventing pregnancy reflect a lot of confusion about "the facts of life." The important thing to remember is that *a girl can become pregnant at any time after she starts having menstrual periods.* What are some of these myths?

"We never go all the way even though we come close to it, so I/she can't get pregnant." Wrong. A girl can get pregnant even if a boy ejaculates just outside her vagina. There's a chance that some of the semen may get into the vagina, and if it does, pregnancy can occur. This isn't common, but it has happened.

"You can't get pregnant if you have intercourse standing up." Wrong. You can get pregnant if you have intercourse standing up, lying down, or sitting in chairs, in cars, in bed, on couches, or on the grass. The place or position doesn't matter. As long as sperm is ejaculated into the vagina, a girl can get pregnant.

"You can only get pregnant right after your period . . . right before your period . . . right in the middle of your cycle . . ." and so forth. Wrong again. A girl can become pregnant at any time of the month. Though women are less likely to get pregnant when they're menstruating, even that has been known to happen.

"He pulls out before he has an orgasm, so I'm safe." No, you're not. Sperm are present in the fluid that's ejaculated during orgasm, but there may also be some in the clear fluid that comes from the penis before orgasm, soon after an erection occurs. So some sperm may enter the vagina even if the boy pulls out before orgasm. And again, it only takes one sperm to cause pregnancy.

"Girls can't get pregnant if they don't have an orgasm." Yes, they can.

"I'll/She'll douche afterwards . . . with vinegar . . . with water . . . with cola . . . with a vaginal douche." Douching, which is flushing the vagina with a liquid, does not prevent pregnancy, no matter what the liquid is. Either sperm have already entered the uterus by the time a girl gets around to douching, or the liquid pushes them up into it. Douching is not an acceptable form of birth control.

"I'll use a tampon." "I'll use plastic wrap." "I'll use a balloon." These all may be great for their original purposes —for absorbing menstrual flow, for keeping food from drying out, for decorating at kids' birthday parties—but none is any good as a contraceptive. And if there's anything else you've heard of that isn't mentioned here, *that* isn't any good either. The only good contraceptive is one that's designed to be a contraceptive.

"It can't happen to me." This is the myth that causes the

most mischief. Few girls would admit that they *really* believe it, but most act as though it's true. The sad fact is that it *can* happen to you, just as it happened to more than one million American teenage girls who became pregnant last year.

Probably the most destructive myth about birth control is that it's not romantic. Actually, the proper use of some method of birth control can make things more romantic, because neither of you has to worry about an unplanned pregnancy. Birth control might make your relationship freer and more spontaneous, rather than less so.

Of course, if you do plan ahead, it means admitting that you're planning on sex, and some teenagers find it difficult to admit that. Girls, more than boys, are the victims of this kind of thinking. Boys often carry condoms in their wallets, "just in case." But girls often feel that planning is wrong— that only unplanned, passionate, "spontaneous" sex is okay. The trouble is that an unplanned, spontaneous pregnancy can be a disaster, and having an unwanted child can be tragic. The business about being overcome by passion is all too often just a way for a girl to let herself avoid facing her own sexuality, desires, and responsibility. Quite simply, if either of you is not ready to think about contraception, you're not ready for intercourse.

Contraception should be the responsibility of both partners. Neither the girl nor the boy should feel that it's up to the other. If you're going to share a sexual experience, you should share the responsibility of preventing an unwanted pregnancy.

There are several effective methods of birth control, and the one you choose should be the one that meets *your* requirements. Each method has both advantages and disadvantages, and no one of them is right for everyone.

The contraceptives most frequently used are the barrier contraceptives, which work by placing some sort of barrier between the sperm and the egg so that pregnancy can't occur. The three barrier contraceptives commonly used are condoms, spermicides, and diaphragms.

Condoms (also called prophylactics, "rubbers," or "Trojans") can help to prevent venereal disease as well as pregnancy. They are, in fact, the single most effective way to prevent the spread of venereal disease, as well as the only approved temporary method of contraception that a male can use. Condoms work by preventing sperm from entering the vagina. After ejaculation, semen remains in the tip of the condom. A condom must be fitted over the penis after it is erect but before intercourse begins. After ejaculation, the boy should remove his penis from the girl's vagina while holding the end of the condom so it doesn't slip off. Condoms should not be reused.

Condoms are readily available in drugstores. More and more stores carry them on open shelves, so you don't have to ask for them. If you do ask a clerk, don't be surprised at the question, "What size, small or large?" The "size" doesn't refer to penis size, but to the number of condoms in a packet, usually three or twelve.

Spermicides are foams, creams, jellies, or suppositories that act to destroy sperm before they can pass through the cervical opening. A spermicide is inserted into a girl's vagina before intercourse. Spermicides are available without a prescription at drugstores. When used with a condom or diaphragm, spermicides are effective; when used as the only method of contraception, they are much less so. Though advertisements for contraceptive suppositories make it sound as if they're as effective as a diaphragm when used by themselves, they are *not,* and should be used with a condom.

All spermicides must be inserted shortly before intercourse. Additional applications are needed every time intercourse is repeated. Foaming tablets and suppositories should be inserted at least fifteen minutes before intercourse. Don't walk around after inserting any spermicide. And remember that no spermicide is considered effective for more than an hour after insertion. Spermicides can inhibit the growth of organisms that cause venereal disease, but, again, they must be used every time intercourse takes place.

The third kind of barrier contraceptive is the diaphragm, a rubber cup that should always be spread with a spermicidal cream or jelly and then placed in the vagina, where it covers the cervical opening and prevents sperm from entering. Diaphragms must be fitted by a doctor and cannot be bought without a prescription. The reason for this is that they come in different sizes, and if a diaphragm doesn't fit properly, it offers no protection. The doctor who fits the diaphragm will explain how to insert it, and will check to see that you know how to do it properly. The size should be rechecked by a doctor once a year—or sooner than that if you've gained or lost fifteen or more pounds, or if you've been pregnant or have had an abortion.

You can put in a diaphragm at any time before intercourse, but if you put it in more than two hours ahead of time, you'll need to reapply the spermicidal cream or jelly. You'll also need more cream or jelly if intercourse is repeated, because each application protects against fertilization from just one ejaculation. Do *not* remove the diaphragm to insert the additional spermicide. To be effective, the diaphragm must be left in place for at least six hours after intercourse. After this, it should be removed, washed with warm water and soap, gently dried, and put away in its container. (Note: Some girls think that a diaphragm can get lost inside the body, but that's impossible because of the way females are built.)

All three of the barrier contraceptives are safe to use and have no side effects. It's possible to be allergic to one of the ingredients in a spermicide and to start itching or get a rash. If this happens, using a different brand may help. Barrier contraceptives are effective if they are used properly; the combination of a condom and a spermicide is especially good. None of these contraceptives is in the least effective if it remains in your wallet, in a drawer, or in the medicine chest. If you're going to use any of the barrier contraceptives, you must be mature enough to realize that it must be used without fail each time you have intercourse. If either of you is unwilling to make that commitment, then the girl should consider having an IUD inserted or taking "the Pill."

An IUD (intrauterine device) is a small, flexible piece of plastic that's inserted into the uterus by a doctor. It remains there at all times. A tiny string tail attached to the main part of the IUD hangs outside the cervix so that you can touch it to make sure the IUD is still in place. An IUD can be expelled from the uterus during menstruation without your noticing it, so you should check after each period to make sure it's still there.

There is still some debate about how an IUD works. It may be that the slight inflammation an IUD sets up prevents a fertilized egg from attaching itself to the wall of the uterus, or it may be that an IUD immobilizes the sperm. Whatever its method of action, an IUD is quite effective. If you're sexually active and careless about using barrier contraceptives, you might want to consider an IUD.

IUDs have disadvantages, however. Insertion may be uncomfortable (though some doctors use a local anesthetic). For the first few months after it's inserted, an IUD may cause heavier-than-usual menstrual flow, cramps, or spotting between periods. These side effects usually disappear. If they continue for longer than two or three months, your doctor may want to remove the IUD. If you have severe pain or tenderness in the abdominal area at any time, check with your doctor immediately.

IUDs have been linked to a greatly increased risk of pelvic infections. Many doctors prefer not to give an IUD to a teenage girl unless there is some overriding reason for her not to use another form of contraception.

"The Pill" is a general term for oral contraceptives. Different brands of the Pill come in different combinations of the hormones estrogen and progesterone, and work in several different ways to prevent pregnancy. Oral contraceptives keep the ovaries from releasing eggs, and also affect the lining of the uterus so that a fertilized egg could not attach itself to the wall of the uterus if fertilization did somehow occur.

Oral contraceptives are available only by prescription. No doctor will prescribe them without giving you a thorough physical examination. At that time, he or she will talk to you about the advantages and disadvantages of taking the Pill.

The Pill is the most effective method of birth control, but it must be taken regularly. Oral contraceptives come packaged either twenty-one or twenty-eight to a packet. If it's a twenty-one-day packet, you take one pill each day for three weeks, then no pills for a week; then the cycle starts again. If it's a twenty-eight-day packet, you take a pill every single day—but only twenty-one of the pills contain hormones; the other seven are either sugar pills or pills containing iron (to make up for the iron lost during menstruation). With either system, menstruation will occur during the week off the hormones, and you're still protected against pregnancy for those seven days. If you forget to take a pill for one or two days, take the ones you forgot along with the regular one for the next day or two, but use a backup barrier contraceptive for the rest of the cycle.

Oral contraceptives have side effects—these can include weight gain (three to five pounds at most), bloating, breast tenderness, and nausea. Usually these side effects can be remedied by changing the brand of pill you use, because each brand contains a different balance of hormones. If any of these side effects bother you, speak to your doctor about changing brands.

Major complications have been associated with the use of the Pill, but many of these problems affect women in their thirties and forties, and new research points to the possibility that the complications were caused by something other than the Pill. The newer oral contraceptives have doses of hormones far lower than those used as recently as ten years ago, and there seem to be fewer complications associated with their use. In older women, there are risks associated with using the Pill and smoking. There's no data yet about possible risks to teenagers who use the Pill and smoke. If you do smoke and are concerned about taking the Pill, keep in mind that smoking is far more hazardous to your health than using the Pill is. If you're going to give up one, give up smoking.

Complications for teenagers on the Pill are minimal, and

the risks of using it as a regular contraceptive are fewer than the risks associated with pregnancy or abortion during the teen years. Some years ago, doctors recommended using the Pill for just a few years and then taking some time off. At this time, there are no such recommendations, and the Pill can be taken continuously. However, you cannot take some of your friend's pills or take one a week, or take one just after intercourse, and expect to be protected against pregnancy. If you're going to go on the Pill, you must take your pills regularly, as prescribed.

If you have intercourse rarely, it's silly to take the Pill. But if you need a contraceptive regularly and don't want to be bothered with barrier methods, then the Pill may well be right for you.

The efficiency of the various birth control methods can be summed up in the following way:

> If 100 couples have intercourse for one year, by the end of the year:
>
> eighty women will be pregnant if they use no contraception
>
> fifteen women will be pregnant if they use spermicide alone
>
> ten women will be pregnant if they use condoms alone
>
> four women will be pregnant if they use the diaphragm and spermicide
>
> three women will be pregnant if they use the IUD

> one or two women will be pregnant if they use con-
> doms and spermicide together
> not even one woman will be pregnant if they use the
> Pill

A method of birth control that requires no physical apparatus or pills is the rhythm method. There are several variations on the rhythm method, but the idea behind all of them is that the woman abstains from sexual intercourse on the days of her menstrual cycle when she is most likely to conceive. The rhythm method is a poor choice of birth control for teenagers, because it's so unreliable. During the teen years, ovulation often isn't regular, and body temperature (which is one way of indicating the time of ovulation) is easily affected by illness or stress.

DES (diethylstilbestrol) is a synthetic estrogen compound that is now used as an *emergency* form of birth control in cases (such as rape) where the use of other methods was impossible. If DES is taken within three days of unprotected intercourse, it will usually prevent pregnancy, because it changes the composition of the lining of the uterus so that a fertilized egg can't implant itself. DES is also known as "the morning-after pill," but it's not one pill, it's a series of fifty tablets taken over five days. Usually the DES treatment makes a woman very nauseated. Its use has also been linked to certain forms of cancer. DES should *never* be considered a regular form of birth control.

Surgical sterilization is a permanent form of birth control

for both men and women, but it is usually considered an alternative for people who have all the children they want. It should not be considered as a possible method of birth control for a teenager.

Any teenager has a right to buy nonprescription contraceptives—that is, condoms and spermicides. At the time of this writing, all family-planning clinics that receive federal funds must offer all contraceptive services without regard to age. It isn't necessary for you to have the consent of your parents to use the services of such a family-planning clinic —nor will the clinic inform your parents if you choose to use its services. How do you find such a clinic? Call Planned Parenthood in your area to see if they have a clinic near you. Look in your phone book in the "Community Services" or "Human Services" section for the category "Birth Control Information" or "Family Planning." Or call the obstetrics and gynecology department at your local hospital to see if they have a clinic. If you want to be certain about a clinic's policy regarding minors, phone and ask them. You need not give your name.

If you're having intercourse, it's possible to become pregnant. Pregnancy occurs when the egg, or ovum, is fertilized by a sperm. When this happens, the fertilized egg enters the uterus and attaches itself to the uterine lining, which is rich in the nutrients needed for growth. If the egg is not fertilized, it enters the uterus and disintegrates. Both the unneeded uterine lining and the egg leave the body in the form of the monthly menstrual flow.

A missed menstrual period is the most common sign of pregnancy, but there are things other than pregnancy that can cause a missed period—they include illness, stress, tension, and sudden weight loss. Sometimes breast tenderness, overwhelming fatigue, nausea and vomiting, and frequent urination are also early signs of pregnancy. If there's any possibility that you're pregnant, you should have a pregnancy test done under a doctor's supervision. A urine test done in a qualified medical laboratory can be done about two weeks after your missed period was due. On the other hand, a blood test done in a qualified medical laboratory is very accurate and can diagnose pregnancy as early as one week after conception. Today, the blood test most frequently used measures levels of HCG (human chorionic gonadotropin), a hormone that is produced at high levels early in pregnancy. Home pregnancy testing kits are now available, but the chance of getting an incorrect result with one of these kits is too high.

The answer you'll get from a pregnancy test is either "positive" or "negative." "Positive" means that you're pregnant, "negative" that you're not.

If you think you may be pregnant, it's vital to have a test done as soon as possible—for two reasons. One is that the first three months of pregnancy are critical to the development of the fetus. The sooner you find out that you're definitely pregnant, the sooner you can start taking the proper steps to insure that the fetus will have the best possible start. The other reason is that if you decide to have an abortion, then the earlier it's done, the safer and easier it is.

If you find yourself pregnant unexpectedly, the decision about what to do is going to be difficult to make, but you're going to have to make it fairly quickly. Find someone to talk to who is not directly involved and who can help you clarify your own thinking about what would be best for you. You can find trained counselors at a mental health facility or a Planned Parenthood center; your own doctor has probably talked to other pregnant teenagers about their options; your clergyman or favorite teacher might be sympathetic. In any case, you need someone to listen to you think out loud, someone who will not tell you what to do, but who will help you explore your options and make a responsible decision about what to do.

It's important to know that abortions are legal in this country, so it's possible to have a safe abortion under medical supervision. This means that not going on with the pregnancy is a choice you can make without having to fear for your physical health. The tragic results of abortions done by untrained people under unsanitary conditions should be a thing of the past. And because legal abortions are safe, under no circumstances consider using herbal teas, hot baths, or any other method you've heard of that's supposed to stop a pregnancy for sure. Don't consider any method of ending a pregnancy other than an abortion by a trained person in a medical facility.

At the time of this writing, a minor (someone under eighteen years of age) can get an abortion during the first trimester (the first three months of pregnancy) without her parents' consent, but laws concerning abortion rights may be changed when you read this. To get the latest information about your rights, call the National Abortion Federation at 800-223-0618. This is a toll-free call—in other words, it won't cost you anything. If you live in New York City, call 688-8516. The National Abortion Federation can also give you information about clinics throughout the country. Or call Planned Parenthood, or your local chapter of the American Civil Liberties Union (ACLU) for information about abortion rights.

Abortions done under medical supervision during the first trimester are very safe. Abortions done at this time are usually done in one of two ways: by vacuum aspiration or by dilatation and curettage (D and C).

In vacuum aspiration, a flexible plastic tube attached to a suction apparatus is inserted into the uterus through the cervix, and the contents of the uterus are removed by suction. In a dilatation and curettage, the doctor scrapes out the lining of the uterus using a curette, a metal loop at the end of a long, thin handle. Both kinds of abortions can be done under local anesthesia, or with general anesthesia if you prefer. Neither method requires an overnight hospital stay. Abortions performed during the second trimester are more complex and require a hospital stay.

The possibility that you've accidentally become pregnant is difficult to face, but the situation won't become any easier if you try to ignore it. If you think you may be pregnant, have a test done as soon as possible. If it's negative, you can stop worrying (and start using a more effective form of contraception). If it's positive, at least you've given yourself more time to explore your options.

Some teenagers find that they are unready for any intense relationship with someone else, but do like to fantasize about what such a relationship would be like. Fantasies are part of living, and without them our lives would be less rich. Most people—children, teenagers, and adults—have fantasies about one thing or another. We call such fantasizing "daydreaming" or "building castles in the air," because we recognize that what we imagine isn't what will really happen, but only what we hope might happen.

It's quite normal for some fantasies to focus on sexual thoughts and desires. Many teenagers feel guilty about fantasizing about sex, but thoughts and fantasies can't hurt you. Thinking about something isn't the same as doing it, and most fantasies are never acted out. No one should feel guilty about fantasies that remain fantasies.

Sexual fantasies often lead to masturbation. Masturbation

is a common and normal human activity practiced by men, women, and children, young and old, single, married, widowed, or divorced. It's a healthy expression of sexuality and can offer release from sexual tensions. Only when masturbation becomes mechanical and a way to avoid dealing with problems or feelings does it become harmful. And then it doesn't harm the body, but the mind.

Masturbation is the direct stimulation of the genitals—the penis for boys, the clitoris for girls. Even young children masturbate—not because it's explicitly sexual, but because it feels pleasurable. After the sexual development of adolescence, masturbation usually becomes linked with sexual feelings and leads to orgasm, the height of sexual excitement. For boys, this usually means ejaculation; orgasm in girls is usually accompanied by a lubrication of the genitals. Both sexes generally feel a throbbing in the genitals and a sense of relaxation.

Whether you masturbate or not, and how often you do it, is a matter of personal choice. It will *not* give you warts, weaken you, cause pimples, bring on disease, make you blind, or predispose you to mental illness. Nor will masturbation harm you physically unless you masturbate with objects that irritate the genitals.

Group masturbation is common among boys during the teen years. There's nothing abnormal about it, and if you participate, it doesn't mean that you're homosexual. A lot of boys don't feel comfortable participating, and there's nothing wrong with that, either. The decision about whether to join in should be a personal one.

At some point during the teen years, nearly every teenager worries that he or she may be homosexual. (A homosexual person is one who has a sexual preference for someone of the same sex.) Such worries may begin after some explicit sexual experience with someone of the same sex, or because of a fantasy or dream involving a sex partner of the same sex. These kinds of events can be frightening if you think they prove that you're homosexual. But they don't.

A homosexual is usually defined as someone who prefers people of the same sex as sex partners *as an adult.* Many teenagers have had isolated homosexual experiences. In fact, one respected study estimates that more than half of all adolescent boys and about one-third of all adolescent girls have had at least one casual homosexual experience. Homosexual experimentation is common during the teen years, because friendships are intense and affection is expressed in many ways. This is the age, too, for crushes on teachers, quite often those of the same sex. And many teenagers feel at ease only with friends of the same sex; because they feel shy and uncomfortable with members of the other sex. But this is often due to incomplete social development, not to homosexuality.

As adults, most people show a mix of what are generally called "masculine" and "feminine" traits. Though these traits should be considered "human," we often give them sex-related labels because of old customs. Being gentle with infants is considered "feminine," for instance—but fathers are usually as gentle with their babies as mothers are. We learn over time that the average person shows both the traits that are traditionally considered masculine and those traditionally considered feminine—regardless of sex. But during the teen years it is easy to feel confused about this, because almost-adult male and female roles are so new.

There certainly are adult men and women who prefer partners of the same sex, and scientists still don't know definitely why or how these preferences develop. But one or two homosexual episodes, or even several, don't mean that you will live the rest of your life as a homosexual. If you have any questions about this aspect of your sexuality, or if you feel uncomfortable about your sexual adjustment, whether it's homosexual or heterosexual, find someone to talk to who has professional training in this area. Your doctor or your guidance counselor at school may be able to recommend someone, or you might call your local mental health center.

Each of us is born male or female—and sexuality is part of our lives from then on. Your teen years should give you a chance to develop your own identity without feeling pushed into decisions you feel uncomfortable with. You need practice at exercising your own judgment so that you can become the kind of adult who is capable of forming mature and lasting relationships.

EMOTIONAL CONCERNS

The teen years are a time of great emotional change as well as a time of great physical change. And no matter how rapid the physical changes are and how uncomfortable they make you feel, you may experience emotional changes and moods that are even more upsetting. Suddenly, you feel a variety of emotions that are in conflict with each other and even seem to contradict one another; they sometimes follow each other so rapidly that it's hard to handle them. You find yourself reacting very emotionally to a situation you would have shrugged off just six months before. You find that you're laughing a lot and crying a lot and feeling frightened more often than you like to admit—and you don't know why.

Because some of these feelings are so new to you, you may

think that no one has ever felt this way before, that you are "different" in some alarming way. But these emotional changes are a normal part of being a teenager, and a natural part of growing up and moving toward independence. Knowing that may not make the feelings any less intense or any easier to deal with. And it doesn't mean you're not unique. But individuals are likely to experience similar feelings in coping with the same problems.

To be in the midst of adolescence is to be suspended somewhere between childhood and adulthood. It's like balancing on a tightrope, with the familiar safety of childhood behind you and the seeming security and independence of adulthood somewhere ahead. That can be exciting, but it's not an easy place to be. Leaving childhood, with its physical and psychological dependence on your parents, can be frightening—and that can be hard for you to admit, even to yourself. There are new situations to face, and you want to make your own choices, but that often means facing the situations and making choices alone.

This all seems overwhelming at times. You may want to be a child again so someone can take care of you, and so someone else can take the responsibility you don't want. Yet you resent any implication that you are still a child or that you're not completely independent in your thoughts and deeds. At the same time, you're not sure you know your own mind yet, because you've scarcely begun to explore it. You feel—rightly—that the way you acted as a child isn't acceptable to you anymore. But you haven't developed an identity to fit in the place of your old childish one, so you don't quite know how to act, or what you really want—or who you really are.

One of the jobs before you, as you grow into adulthood, is to gather together all the pieces of your personality, sort out what's important to you and what is not, and fit the parts into a single whole. All of this is confusing and often seems to be too much. Of course, most teenagers don't sit down and think it through in that way. What usually happens is that they go through periods of moodiness (the moods varying from elation to depression) as they struggle with this task. The intensity of these moods can be frightening—so frightening, in fact, that teenagers sometimes fear they're going crazy. Usually they're not—they're just coming to grips with the unavoidable difficulties of growing up, with the tremendous tasks of sorting out priorities and personalities and learning to take charge of their own lives.

Depression is probably one of the most frightening emotions of adolescence, and it's important to distinguish between feeling depressed at times, and serious, long-term depression. People often say they feel "depressed" when they are only sad or disappointed. Such feelings are usually reactions to a specific event or situation, such as failing an exam or having a friend move away, and they subside eventually. In real depression, the feelings of despair and sadness aren't based on anything specific, so they last and last regardless of what happens, casting a cloud of gloom over every situation.

Depression is usually triggered by a loss, and teenagers suffer many losses in the process of becoming adults. Some of these losses are obvious—for instance, the loss of a boy friend or girl friend when a romance breaks up. Some other losses are less obvious, though they're losses all the same. One of these is the loss of your childhood identity. No matter how much you looked forward to growing up and gaining the rights and responsibilities of a teenager, when you were a child you knew what to expect from yourself and your parents. Now you begin to question your parents' values as you seek to establish your own. And until you work out your own identity, moral sense, and code of values, you may feel the loss of childhood security very strongly. During this time, it's also easy to lose your self-esteem. The teen years are a time to try out new roles and activities, and since it's hard to do something right the very first time, you're vulnerable to failure and to feelings of worthlessness. Some teenagers react to failure more sharply than others, and this doesn't always depend on how well they perform.

It's natural to feel angry when you lose something important, and anger is part of depression. But in depression your anger is turned inward, back against yourself, instead of being expressed. People who are depressed often believe that their anger is so terrifying that it can't be allowed to come to the surface. But depression is difficult to deal with unless the anger is expressed in some acceptable way.

There's nothing wrong with feeling depressed or moody occasionally if you're reacting to a specific event and your "down" mood passes in a short while. Everyone feels that way sometimes. But if the depression doesn't leave you, if it dominates your thinking and interferes with the way you function for long periods of time, then it's time to do something about it.

How can you tell whether you're suffering from a depression serious enough to require professional help? If the world doesn't start looking a little better within a week; if you stop eating normally and lose a lot of weight without trying to, or if you start overeating; if you turn down invitations even though you have nothing else to do; if you stop combing your hair, taking showers or baths, or paying attention to your clothes because "it just isn't worth it"; if you can't make the simplest decision; or if you feel numb all the time and don't react emotionally even when you think you should—it's time to ask for help.

The first thing to do is to go to your doctor for a checkup. There are several physical conditions that contribute to depression, among them flu, hepatitis, and infectious mononucleosis. If none of these is the cause, and your doctor finds you to be in good health, he or she may be able to recommend a professional therapist or clinic experienced in treating teenagers. Your treatment can be individual or in a group, depending on what's available in your area and what you feel most comfortable with. If your doctor doesn't know of anyone to suggest, look up "Mental Health" or "Social Service Organizations" in the "Community Services" section or Yellow Pages of your telephone book, and call a clinic listed there.

If the hopeless feelings that are part of depression aren't dealt with, they may lead to suicide or suicide attempts. During the teen years, it's not unusual to feel as if you want to commit suicide. But it is a sign that you may not be able to cope with your own feelings and that you need help. When a teenager attempts suicide, he or she isn't really wishing for death, but is saying, in effect, "Help! I want to get out of this situation. I want things to be different."

There are certain warning signs you should be aware of. If a friend threatens suicide, take it seriously. Don't assume that anyone who talks about suicide won't try it; that's a myth. Most people who commit suicide or try to commit suicide tell someone about it before they act. If a friend suddenly starts giving away favorite possessions, such as records, books, or clothing, without apparent reason, it may be a sign that he or she is thinking of suicide. Another warning sign is a sudden change in eating or sleeping patterns. And if your friend starts talking about how easy it would be to commit suicide with the knife/pills/revolver he or she owns, again, take it seriously.

If you don't want to talk to your friend's parents, find some other adult to talk to immediately. It might be the doctor on call at your hospital emergency room, a teacher you trust, an athletic coach, a minister or rabbi, or a neighbor. But don't think that your friend's mood will pass with time. This is an emergency and should be treated as such.

Anxiety is another troubling emotion that's common during the teen years. Anxiety feels like fear, and the two produce similar physical symptoms. But fear is a reaction to a specific threat, while anxiety is a feeling of foreboding not connected to any particular danger. The physical symptoms that accompany both fear and anxiety may include sweating, tenseness, nausea, diarrhea, pounding heart, and shallow breathing.

Everyone feels anxious occasionally, without knowing why. Feelings of anxiety are not abnormal and shouldn't cause any concern unless they occur so frequently that they interfere with day-to-day activities.

How do you know what's "normal" anxiety and what's "abnormal" anxiety? Normal anxiety is the emotion that keys you up before an exam or an athletic competition so that you do your best. Your anxiety is out of bounds if you freeze up with worry so that you can't study or can't react.

Sometimes feelings of anxiety can overcome you without bearing any relation to activities or exams. The panic becomes so strong that you can't get through a day without feeling that something awful is about to happen. Your body may react in different ways to constant, intense anxiety. Because you're always tense, you may have trouble falling asleep at night even though you're tired. Because you know you should sleep, you become more anxious about not sleeping, and you're even more tired the next day. Overbreathing, or hyperventilation, is another common reaction to anxiety. When a person overbreathes, too much air circulates through the lungs, lessening the level of carbon dioxide in the body so that it's below normal. This results in physical symptoms that include not being able to take a deep breath, feeling that you're not getting enough air, light-headedness, and a tingling or numbness in the hands or fingers.

Sometimes you may feel as if you're going to faint during an overbreathing episode, or even as if you might die. It's possible to be so worried about feeling light-headed that you don't realize you're breathing rapidly and shallowly. Once you recognize what's happening, you can make a conscious effort to slow down your breathing and take deeper breaths. It sometimes helps to breathe in and out of a paper bag if you're starting to overbreathe. This increases the level of carbon dioxide in the body and brings it back to normal.

Headache is another way your body copes with stress. Not all headaches are emotional in origin, of course. Colds, flu, sinus infections, allergies, or eye strain all may cause headaches. If you suffer from headaches regularly, you should see a doctor. If the headaches are not the result of a specific physical problem, they are usually the result of a combination of emotional and physical strains.

Tension headaches occur frequently in teenagers. The headache is caused by muscle tension, and is usually felt across the forehead, as a band around the head, or on both sides of the head. Typically, a tension headache develops slowly as the day wears on. The muscles that caused the headache may remain tender after the headache is gone. Heating pads, massage, and aspirin or aspirin substitutes usually help, but they're only part of the answer. The headache is a symptom of a stressful condition, so it's necessary to find the source of the stress and deal with that.

Headaches may also be caused by depression or anxiety. While tension headaches develop during the day and usually occur on school days, headaches brought on by depression or anxiety are likely to occur in the morning, in the evening, or on weekends. Like tension headaches, they have roots in emotions and are physical responses to the emotions.

Migraine headaches are usually felt only on one side of the head. Migraines are not simply headaches, but may be regarded as a disease. Migraines seem to run in families. Typically, there are physical symptoms that occur before the headache starts, and other physical symptoms that accompany the headache.

Migraine sufferers usually have altered vision, known as an "aura," before the headache starts. The aura sometimes takes the form of dancing lights, or a blind spot in one eye, or flashing colors. Then the headache starts as a throbbing pain. It is generally accompanied by sensitivity to light and noise and by nausea, and it may be accompanied by vomiting.

Migraines can be treated effectively, so if you get them, make an appointment to see your doctor about them. There's no need to suffer through them without help.

Because the emotional changes of the teen years are so intense, you may feel that you can't get through some of the most distressing times without help. All you may need to do is talk to a close friend. Or you may want to talk to an adult friend of the family, an older brother or sister, your parents, a teacher, your doctor, or your minister or rabbi. If you trust the person's good sense and affection for you, talking about your feelings may give you a new perspective.

You may prefer to talk to someone who is professionally trained to help people deal with their problems. You can find a professional counselor by looking under "Mental Health" or "Social Service Organizations" in the "Community Services" section or Yellow Pages of your telephone book. If you do see a professional counselor, anything you say will remain confidential unless you specifically give your permission for the counselor to tell someone else. You needn't be "weird" or "around the bend" to seek help from a professional. You just have to admit that you have problems you can't solve by yourself. Together, you and a counselor can make sense of what's troubling you and figure out what to do about it.

ROLES AND RIGHTS
AS PATIENTS

When you were a child, you probably visited your doctor regularly for inoculations and routine examinations. During those years, your visits were scheduled at regular intervals so that your doctor could make certain that you were growing and gaining weight normally, and that any minor problem could be dealt with before it became major. But now that you're in your teens, you may not think you need to visit a doctor unless you become seriously ill. Because routine inoculations are usually completed and schools often don't require physical examinations each year, many teenagers don't see a doctor for two or three or even four years at a time. But because your body is changing so rapidly, a regular checkup is vital to your health. A routine physical examination once a year during the teen years is one of the best ways of keeping a minor physical ailment from becoming serious.

It's important that you feel comfortable with your doctor. When you were young, your parents chose the doctor you would see because *they* trusted him or her to care for you. Now that you'll be taking more responsibility for your own care, you should have a doctor with whom *you* can feel a sense of trust. Many family doctors take pride in treating patients from infancy to adulthood, and there's no reason to change doctors simply because you've reached your teens. If you like the doctor you've been seeing since you were a child and he or she also treats teenagers, that's fine. Some pediatricians (doctors who specialize in treating children) are also trained to treat teenagers, so you may want to continue with your childhood doctor. But if you're the only teenager in a waiting room full of infants, you may feel awkward. If you feel uncomfortable continuing to see the doctor who treated you when you were a child, you can be honest about it and ask for the names of doctors in your area who see teenagers. It's not likely that your doctor will be insulted by such a request.

If visiting a private doctor is out of the question because of expense, you can find a clinic that specializes in treating teenagers for very low fees or no fee at all. These clinics are usually listed in the Yellow Pages of your telephone book under "Medical Services" or "Clinics." If there isn't one listed in your telephone book, you can call your city or state health department or the pediatrics department of the nearest medical school and ask for the location of a nearby clinic treating teenagers.

It's important to keep in mind that the relationship between doctor and patient is two-sided. Though the doctor has been professionally trained to keep people in good health and to treat illness, you are the expert on yourself. As such, you have certain responsibilities as a patient. If you don't fulfill them, you can't expect your doctor to do his or her best for you.

One of your responsibilities is to be honest with your doctor. To help diagnose your problem and prescribe treatment correctly, your doctor will ask a number of questions. If you don't answer honestly, you make it harder for the doctor to treat you.

As a patient, you also have the right—and the responsibility—to ask questions. Don't be afraid that you're wasting your doctor's time, or that he or she will think you're stupid if you don't understand something. Most doctors want you to ask questions, because a patient who understands what's happening is more likely to follow instructions about treatment and medications. If you don't understand what the doctor is saying, ask him or her to repeat it more slowly or to explain it more clearly. And don't expect your doctor to be able to read your mind. He or she can't answer your question if you don't ask it.

Most people are embarrassed to talk about some subjects with their doctors. But no matter what the question, your doctor has heard it before. If you feel that certain questions will be difficult for you to ask, write a list before you go to the office. Somehow it's easier to read something from a list, and making a list guarantees that you won't forget all the questions you've thought of asking. If your doctor is someone you feel you could never talk to about some subjects, then maybe you should consider seeing a different doctor.

There are certain standard procedures you can expect in a typical physical examination. If this is your first visit, your doctor will want a complete medical history. You'll be asked a series of questions about your health and your family's health. The doctor will want to know about childhood illnesses and about problems such as headaches, dizziness, colds, and sore throats. He or she will also ask about any diseases that run in your family—for example, diabetes, cancer, heart disease—and about allergies, immunizations, and any medicines you may be taking. Your answers to these questions will give the doctor a general picture of your physical condition.

In taking your medical history, your doctor may use some medical terms or disease names that you don't understand. If you do have trouble with any of the questions, ask your doctor to explain in simpler language. Doctors sometimes forget that most people don't use medical terms every day, and there is no medical phrase or medical condition that can't be explained in everyday language.

Your doctor may also talk to you about school, your friends, your vacation plans, and the sports that interest you. This may seem to have nothing to do with your physical health, but it's important for your doctor to get a sense of your everyday life. A good relationship with a doctor requires that he or she treat you as a person, not as a collection of symptoms and test results. Your outside interests, school, and friends all influence who you are as a person. So don't think it odd if you find yourself talking about the latest baseball results or today's headlines or local politics when you go in for a physical checkup.

After you give your medical history, your doctor will examine you. If this is your first visit, the physical examination will be especially thorough. A complete checkup covers certain basic items, but your doctor will not necessarily perform the tests and go through the examination in exactly the order described below.

Before you go into the examining room, you'll be asked to leave a urine specimen in a paper or plastic cup. You don't have to fill the cup completely; fill it about one-third to one-half full and let the rest of the urine run into the toilet. Girls collect urine specimens by sitting on the toilet and holding the cup under them.

Urine is used for several different tests—to make sure that

your kidneys and bladder are functioning properly; to see whether there are bacteria or blood cells in the urine that would signal the presence of a disease; and to check for normal levels of sugar and protein.

After you leave a urine specimen, you'll be given an examining gown and asked to put it on. It's usually put on so that it ties in the back. You'll be left alone to get undressed; most offices have hangers or a chair for your clothes.

When you're ready, the doctor, physician's assistant, or nurse will measure your height, weigh you, and take your blood pressure. Having your blood pressure taken doesn't hurt. A pressure cuff is wrapped around your upper arm and pumped up with air. Your pulse is measured as the pressure is released.

When your heart beats, it pumps blood first into the aorta, the largest artery in the body. From there, the blood is pumped through the body's arteries until it finally reaches the smallest blood vessels, called capillaries. The flow of blood meets some resistance from all these vessels. Your blood pressure measures this resistance.

Blood pressure is written as two numbers—130/70, for instance. The first number represents systolic pressure—that is, the amount of force under which blood is sent from the heart to the aorta. The second number represents diastolic pressure—that is, the amount of force required to send blood into the capillaries against the resistance it meets. The more force needed, the higher the reading.

Average blood pressure for teenagers ranges between 120/70 and 140/80, but both lower and higher readings may be normal. Your blood pressure can be affected temporarily by illness, tension, or exercise. If you rushed in to your appointment or were a little scared of having your blood pressure taken, it probably will be artificially high, and your doctor might want to take it again before you leave.

After you've been weighed, measured, and had your blood pressure taken, your doctor will look over your body one area at a time. Starting at your head, he or she will check for hair loss or changes in hair texture that might indicate some specific disease. Next, your eyes are examined; the doctor will use a light that allows him or her to see the retina and the blood cells that supply it. (Sometimes high blood pressure and diabetes can be diagnosed through an eye examination.) Your doctor will also check for weak eye muscles by having you follow a moving finger with your eyes, and by asking you to focus first on something nearby and then on something across the room.

Your ears, nose, and mouth will be examined for any abnormalities or signs of disease. Your doctor will then feel around your neck and under your arms for swelling of the lymph glands, which could signal that your white blood cells are working to fight some disease. A lot of people are ticklish around the neck and arms. If you are, don't be afraid to laugh; you won't be the only one who's ever done it. Your doctor will finish as quickly as possible.

Your chest area will be examined next. Your doctor will check to see that your heart and lungs are normal by listening with a stethoscope and by tapping your chest and back. He or she is alert for any signs of asthma, pneumonia, or other lung disease at this point in the examination. With girls, a breast examination will show up any lumps or other abnormalities of breast tissue. Cancer of the breast is extremely rare in teenage girls, but it's a good idea to ask your doctor to show you how to examine your own breasts so that you can get into the habit of self-examination now and make it a regular part of your monthly routine.

Your abdominal area will be examined next. Your liver and spleen will be checked for size and tenderness. Try to relax during this part of the examination, because tense muscles make it harder for your doctor to examine you accurately.

Next, the doctor will check your genitals. With boys, this means examining the penis and testes for any rashes or abnormalities. With girls, it sometimes means an internal examination. Some doctors think an internal examination is unnecessary for younger teenage girls. If your doctor believes an internal examination should be done, a female nurse or physician's assistant should be present if the doctor is a man. If the doctor is a woman, no one else has to be present.

In an internal examination, the doctor uses a speculum, a special instrument designed to hold the vagina open so that he or she can see the cervix clearly and check it for signs of anything abnormal. With the speculum in place, the doctor may take a sample of cervical cells for a Pap smear. This doesn't hurt at all, because a blunt wooden or cotton-tipped swab is used. The sample is sent to a laboratory to be tested for the presence of abnormal or precancerous cells.

After the speculum is removed, the doctor will put on a thin rubber glove, lubricate his or her fingers with special cream, and insert one or two fingers into your vagina while placing the other hand on your abdomen and gently pressing down. This discloses the size and shape of your uterus, ovaries, and oviducts.

After the genital examination, the doctor will usually do a rectal examination. Wearing a rubber glove lubricated with a special cream, he or she inserts a finger into the anus to check for swelling or lumps. A rectal examination will disclose any splits in the skin of the rectum, and any hemorrhoids.

Finally, the doctor will check your arms and legs for any signs of swelling or bone problems, and your spine for abnormal curvature.

At some point, your doctor will take a sample of blood from your arm for a blood test. No one *likes* having blood samples taken, so you don't have to feel silly about being afraid. It helps to look the other way; the whole procedure takes only a few seconds. A blood test is important because it's a way of checking for anemia and hepatitis, as well as other diseases.

After your doctor has finished examining you, he or she will leave the room so that you can get dressed in private. Some doctors then meet with you to talk about the physical findings; others will talk about them during the examination and won't see you afterwards unless you have some questions. If there's anything about the examination you didn't understand, want to talk about, or need more information about, now is the time to talk to the doctor. Don't think that your concerns are a bother to the doctor, or that you'll take up too much of his or her valuable time. It is, after all, your body and your health.

One thing most teenagers are concerned about is whether what they say to a doctor will be kept confidential. If you are being treated by a private doctor, there are no laws that say he or she cannot speak with your parents—and the doctor may feel required to do so, especially if your parents are paying your medical bills. If you're concerned about this, ask your doctor, "Are my visits here considered confidential?" Most doctors will respect your request that no information be passed on without your consent, and will ask your permission to talk with your parents if they feel it's necessary to do so.

At the time of this writing, there are some specific instances in which you can get medical help without your parents' consent, and without having to worry that your parents will be notified. If you're being treated for drug abuse at a clinic or a hospital drug-abuse unit, strict federal laws protect your privacy. If you're being treated or tested for venereal disease at a city or state health department clinic, your visits will be confidential. Most clinics will not notify your parents if you seek prescription contraceptives. But just to be sure, call the clinic to ask about their policy. Laws concerning your rights to an abortion are under review at this time, so call Planned Parenthood, or your local chapter of the American Civil Liberties Union (ACLU), or the National Abortion Federation for up-to-date information.

INDEX